ILLUSTRATED LIBRARY OF COOKING

VOLUME 12 Pas-Pie

Calling all pasta, pastry and pie lovers. Paging everyone who longingly remembers the Good Old Days. Included here you'll find a treasury of classic pasta recipes, another of absolutely scrumptious non-pie pastries (that means cream puffs, eclairs, strudels, Napoleons). There are pies, too. By the dozen. And a sampler of old-time dishes.

ROCKVILLE HOUSE PUBLISHERS, INC
ROCKVILLE CENTRE, NEW YORK 11570

VOLUME **12**

Family Circle®

Illustrated Library of

COOKING

YOUR READY REFERENCE FOR A LIFETIME OF GOOD EATING

Table of Contents

PASTA AND RICE:
INTRODUCING THE PASTA FAMILY, A QUICK DICTIONARY OF POPULAR PASTA, SOME PASTA DISHES AND SAUCES, ALL ABOUT RICE, FOUR RICE DESSERTS

History lives in pasta and in rice. Rice, in fact, was one of man's earliest and most important foods. It originated not in China as most of us believe, but in the Indus Valley of ancient Babylonia. Buddha, it is said, once lived on a single grain of rice a day. Perhaps. Certainly, Buddhists were responsible for spreading the use of rice throughout the Orient, for making it a daily staple.

Another Oriental staple was a sort of pasta. Not the sturdy starchy fare we know today, but thin transparent noodles made of rice flour paste (they are popular still in Chinese cuisine). Some believe that this was the original pasta, that Marco Polo sampled it while in the East, liked it and carried it home to Italy. Others believe that Italians were making pasta pre-Marco Polo, a type very similar to that popular today.

Whatever its origin, pasta has been an everyday food in Italy for hundreds of years. Before the dawn of the Renaissance, Italian cooks were making a flour-and-egg dough that they rolled and cut into vermicelli, then boiled in cauldrons. By the mid-Renaissance this nourishing pasta was the popular staple of peasant and patrician alike. By the end of the 15th century it was being made commercially. Catherine de' Medici made pasta fashionable in France and soon all of Europe was trying to duplicate the recipes being served at the French court.

It was no less a man than Thomas Jefferson who introduced pasta to America by serving spaghetti at a formal White House dinner. Jefferson also brought rice to America, smuggling a few grains of it home from a trip abroad. He had the grains planted in the South Carolina low country around Charleston; the plants flourished, and rice became one of young America's money-makers.

Today, of course, both pasta and rice are great favorites across America. They are economical, enormously versatile because they partner equally well with meat, fish, fowl and vegetables, and they are unusually easy to prepare. The following recipes prove just *how* easy.

1415

INTRODUCING THE PASTA FAMILY

Shopping for pasta is a treasure hunt, as this ever-growing food group—including spaghetti, macaroni and noodles—adds up to more than 150 varieties. Among them you'll find plain and fancy shapes; big and little sizes; packaged, canned and frozen specialties, all costing just pennies a serving. Notes here show why good cooks count on pasta.

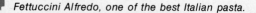
Fettuccini Alfredo, one of the best Italian pasta.

Variety Unlimited:

Take a few extra minutes to look over the various kinds of pasta that your supermarket offers, as there is almost no end to the ways you can use them for family and party meals. Their mild wheaty flavor gives an appealing heartiness to main dishes, casseroles, soups and salads. And what would we do without pasta to stretch a yesterday's roast or a little cheese! Sizes and shapes include long and short, jumbo and bitsy, thin and chubby, hollow and flat, twists, shells, spirals, rings—even novelties to please the children. (The chart that follows describes many popular kinds, including the meanings of the fanciful Italian names.) Today most pasta is vitamin-enriched, as our breads are. And noodles marked EGG have the goodness of yolks added. Look for these enrichment pluses on the label; they are your guarantee you are getting good food value for your money.

Sleight-of-Hand Cooking:

If you're planning favorite macaroni and cheese for dinner, but find you have no elbow macaroni on hand, take heart, since spaghetti, noodles, shells, butterflies, spirals—even mix them if you like—will taste just as good. And it's fun to experiment. When making substitutions, a good guide to remember is that small shapes are perfect for soups, medium sizes mix well in a casserole and the larger thicker types are enjoyed at their best when layered or stuffed or served with sauces.

How Much Should You Buy?

This handy chart shows how much some of the most popular kinds will make when cooked.

1416

Variety (8 ounces)	Uncooked	Cooked
Macaroni (unbroken)	—	4 cups
Spaghetti (unbroken)	—	4 cups
Elbow Macaroni	2 cups	4 cups
Rotelle (spirals)	4 cups	4 cups
Farfalle (butterflies)	5 cups	4 cups
Shells (small)	2 cups	4 cups
Noodles (wide and regular)	6 cups	3½ cups
Noodles (fine)	5 cups	5½ cups

About Instants and Mixes:

It's good menu insurance to have some of the dependable canned, packaged or frozen pasta dishes on hand for days when dinner must be on in a rush. A few choices are:
- Packaged spaghetti and lasagna dinners with canned sauce or sauce mix and cheese. Faster still are the canned macaroni and spaghetti combinations that need heating only.
- Packaged noodle, macaroni and macaroni-rice combinations with seasoning mixes and toppings.
- Canned spaghetti with tomato, mushroom or cheese sauce—some with meat.
- Canned, packaged and frozen fancies including ravioli, lasagna, stuffed manicotti, tuna-noodle casseroles.

A QUICK DICTIONARY OF POPULAR PASTA

Elbow Macaroni—Most popular choice for soups, casseroles and favorite macaroni with cheese. Shown are three sizes, packed in several size "window" boxes and in transparent bags.

Fusilli—New twist on spaghetti. Each strand is curled dizzily and keeps its shape when cooked. Feature it for a spaghetti party, or serve with buttery cheese sauce as the "potato" of the meal.

Rotelle (spirals) and **Farfalle** (butterflies or bows)—Fancy shapes that give any dish a different look. Serve with cheese, mushroom or olive-oil sauce, or use in chowders and salads.

Shells—Available in varying sizes, some as dainty as tiny sea shells. Serve them hot with clam, tuna or cheese sauce, or mix with lobster, crab or shrimps for a hearty main-dish salad.

Macaroni and **Spaghetti**—The most familiar variety of pasta. Macaroni comes in long thick to thin tubelike and flat strands. Spaghetti is a solid thin strand; spaghettini is even thinner.

Noodles—Three widths—wide, medium and fine (also known as vermicelli). All are packed in see-through boxes and bags, the same as elbow macaroni. Most have egg added for color and richness.

Manicotti (muffs) and **Lasagna**—Famous Italian specialties. Cheese stuffing goes inside the big hollow muffs; three cheeses are layered with the lasagna. Both bake in tomato sauce.

Alphabets and **Pastina**—Miniature favorites of children. Alphabets are used mostly in soups; pastina (meaning little dough) is delicious served with milk or turned into a light dessert.

QUICK Q AND A ON PASTA

Q. How long will macaroni keep in its package?

A. Unopened, it should stay fresh for months when stored in a dry cool cupboard. Once it's opened, however, it is best to keep any left in a covered glass or metal container or a sealed plastic bag and use soon. Especially in hot weather, it pays to check your supply for freshness.

Q. Is it necessary to rinse spaghetti or noodles after cooking?

A. No. In fact it is better not to, unless you want to cool them quickly when making a salad. You will notice that package directions suggest cooking in *lots* of rapidly boiling water, which keeps the strands from sticking.

Q. Whenever we order spaghetti in a restaurant, it's firm yet so tasty. How is it cooked?

A. It's a matter of watching boiling time and stopping when spaghetti is tender yet chewy. Italians call this stage of doneness *al dente*.

Q. Is macaroni fattening?

A. No single food actually is fattening. It's the amount and what you put with it that runs up calories—and sometimes fast! A one-cup serving of plain cooked spaghetti or macaroni is about 150 calories.

HOW TO COOK PASTA

A big kettle is best when cooking any pasta, as pasta needs plenty of room to bubble about in to cook evenly without sticking together. For easy handling, cook not more than 1 pound at a time. Water should be boiling merrily before pasta is added, so put it on to heat early (3 quarts of cold water may take as long as 15 minutes to heat to boiling). Follow label directions for salting and cooking time (a few drops of vegetable oil or olive oil added to water help to keep it from boiling over). When cooking long macaroni or spaghetti, hold a handful at one end and lower the other end into the bubbling water until it softens enough to fit into the kettle.

As soon as your pasta is done, pour it into a colander to drain. Then, if it must stand, coat with a little oil or butter or margarine; cover colander lightly and set over kettle with about a 1-inch depth of simmering water. Use kitchen tongs to dish up spaghetti.

Spaghetti Ragout
Makes 6 servings

    4 slices bacon, diced
    1 pound ground beef
    1 medium-size onion, peeled and sliced
    ½ cup sliced celery
    1 medium-size carrot, pared and sliced
    ¼ pound chicken livers, coarsely chopped
    ¼ cup catsup
    2 envelopes instant beef broth
       OR: 2 beef-flavor bouillon cubes
    1½ cups water
    ½ teaspoon salt
    ⅛ teaspoon ground nutmeg
    ½ cup cream for whipping
    ½ pound spaghetti
       Grated Parmesan cheese

1 Sauté bacon until crisp in a large frying pan; add ground beef, onion, celery and carrot. Brown meat, breaking it up as it cooks.
2 Stir in chicken livers, catsup, instant beef broth or bouillon cubes, water, salt and nutmeg, crushing cubes, if using, with a spoon; cover.
3 Simmer, stirring several times, 30 minutes. Blend in cream slowly; heat just until bubbly.
4 While sauce simmers, cook spaghetti, following label directions; drain. Pour sauce over; toss lightly to mix. Serve with Parmesan cheese to sprinkle over.

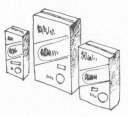

Spaghetti and Meat Balls
Makes 4 servings

    1 pound spaghetti
    2 envelopes spaghetti-sauce mix
    2 cans (8 ounces each) tomato sauce
    3 cups water
    ¼ cup vegetable oil
    1 pound ground beef
    1 small onion, grated
    ¼ cup chopped parsley
    1 egg
    ½ cup ready-mix bread stuffing
    1 teaspoon salt
    ⅛ teaspoon leaf marjoram, crumbled
       Grated Parmesan cheese

1 Cook spaghetti, following label directions; drain.
2 Combine spaghetti-sauce mix, tomato sauce,

1417

water and vegetable oil in a large frying pan; simmer 15 minutes to blend flavors.

3 Mix ground beef lightly with onion, parsley, egg, bread stuffing, salt and marjoram until well blended; shape into 24 balls. Place in hot sauce.

4 Simmer 10 minutes, or until cooked through.

5 Layer cooked spaghetti and meat balls and sauce onto a deep serving platter; serve with Parmesan cheese to sprinkle over.

Spaghetti with Meat Sauce
Makes 12 servings

1 large onion, chopped (1 cup)
2 cloves garlic, minced
¼ cup olive oil or vegetable oil
2 pounds ground beef
2 cans (about 2 pounds each) Italian tomatoes
2 cans (6 ounces each) tomato paste
1 cup water
½ cup chopped celery
¼ cup chopped parsley
2 bay leaves
1 teaspoon leaf basil, crumbled
4 teaspoons salt
2 teaspoons sugar
¼ teaspoon pepper
2 pounds spaghetti
    Grated Parmesan cheese

1 Sauté onion and garlic in olive oil or vegetable oil just until onion is soft in a kettle or Dutch oven; push to one side.

2 Shape ground beef into a large patty in same kettle; brown 5 minutes on each side, then break up into chunks. Stir in remaining ingredients, except spaghetti and cheese.

3 Simmer, stirring several times, 2 hours, or until sauce is thick. Let stand 5 to 10 minutes until fat rises to top, then skim off; remove bay leaves.

4 Cook spaghetti in two kettles, following label directions; drain.

5 Spoon cooked spaghetti and meat sauce into separate large bowls for everyone to dish up his own; serve with grated Parmesan cheese to sprinkle on top.

1418

Spaghetti with Red Clam Sauce
A good party idea for a crowd: Make up a batch of this sauce and one with meat so everybody may take his choice.
Makes 8 servings

1 large onion, chopped (1 cup)
1 clove garlic, minced
¼ cup olive oil or vegetable oil
1 can (about 2 pounds) Italian tomatoes
1 can (8 ounces) tomato sauce
1 can (6 ounces) tomato paste
2 cans (8 ounces each) minced clams
2 teaspoons sugar
2 teaspoons salt
1 teaspoon leaf basil, crumbled
1 teaspoon leaf oregano, crumbled
¼ cup chopped parsley
1 pound spaghetti
    Freshly grated Parmesan cheese

1 Sauté onion and garlic in olive oil or vegetable oil until soft in a large frying pan. Stir in tomatoes, tomato sauce and paste, liquid from clams, sugar, salt, basil and oregano.

2 Simmer, uncovered, stirring often, 1 hour, or until very thick; stir in clams and parsley.

3 While sauce simmers, cook spaghetti in boiling salted water, following label directions; drain. Spoon into a large shallow bowl.

4 Top with clam sauce; toss to mix well. Serve Parmesan cheese separately to sprinkle on top.

Spaghetti with White Clam Sauce
Another favorite sauce with clams. Cooks fast, too!
Makes 4 servings

2 cloves of garlic, minced
4 tablespoons (½ stick) butter or margarine
2 cans (7 ounces each) minced clams
1 cup chopped parsley
1 teaspoon lemon juice
    Dash of cayenne pepper
½ pound spaghettini, cooked and drained

1 Sauté garlic lightly in butter or margarine in medium-size saucepan; stir in clams and juice, parsley, lemon juice and cayenne; simmer 5 minutes.

2 Toss with hot spaghetti; serve plain or with your favorite grated cheese.

Spaghetti Carbonara
Try bacon and eggs this favorite Italian style and discover a double-quick supper dish.
Makes 6 servings

1 pound spaghetti
½ pound sliced bacon, diced
1 large green pepper, halved, seeded and diced
3 eggs
½ teaspoon leaf marjoram, crumbled
½ teaspoon salt

Spaghetti and Meat Balls, everyone's favorite. It's layered here for a dressy appearance but the flavor is earthy and robust. The perfect accompaniment, a just-tossed green salad.

Dash of pepper
4 tablespoons (½ stick) butter or margarine
1 cup grated Romano cheese

1 Cook spaghetti in boiling salted water, following label directions; drain and place on heated serving platter.
2 While pasta cooks, fry bacon until crisp in a skillet. Remove with a slotted spoon to paper toweling. Drain off all but 2 tablespoons bacon fat from skillet. Sauté green pepper in skillet until soft.
3 Beat eggs in a small bowl. Stir in marjoram, salt and pepper.
4 Toss butter or margarine with hot spaghetti until melted. Add seasoned eggs and toss until completely blended. Add bacon, green pepper

and grated cheese. Toss once more and serve at once.

Made-by-You Ravioli
This takes a little time and effort, but it is really worth the work.
Makes 48 ravioli or 6 to 8 servings

3 cups sifted all-purpose flour
2 teaspoons salt
3 eggs
2 tablespoons olive oil or vegetable oil
¼ cup water
    RICOTTA FILLING (recipe follows)
    HOMEMADE TOMATO SAUCE (recipe follows)
½ cup freshly grated Parmesan cheese

1 Sift flour and salt onto a large wooden board; make a well in center; add eggs, oil and water. Work liquids into flour with fingers to make a stiff dough. (Or make dough in a large bowl, but it's not as much fun.)

2 Knead dough on board (do not add additional flour) 10 minutes, or until dough is smooth and soft as perfectly kneaded bread dough.

3 Wrap dough in transparent wrap. Let stand 15 minutes. Cut into quarters; keep dough you are not working with wrapped, or it will dry out.

4 Roll out dough, one quarter at a time on the wooden board (do not use additional flour) to a rectangle, 12x4½. This takes a lot of pressure with rolling pin. Repeat with remaining quarters of dough.

5 Shape ravioli, following directions with Ravioli Form and fill with RICOTTA FILLING. Or: Place 12 teaspoonfuls of filling, evenly spaced, on one rolled-out strip. Cover with a second rolled-out strip and cut between mounds of filling with a fluted pastry wheel. (Ravioli can be cooked at once or placed in a single layer on cookie sheets until ready to cook.)

6 Heat 6 quarts of water to boiling in a kettle; add 2 tablespoons salt and 1 tablespoon oil. Cook ravioli, 24 at a time, 10 minutes; remove with slotted spoon to heated serving dish; top with half the HOMEMADE TOMATO SAUCE and grated Parmesan cheese. Repeat with remaining ravioli, sauce and cheese.

Ricotta Filling
Makes enough to fill 48 ravioli

1 cup ricotta cheese
    OR: 1 container (8 ounces) cream-style cottage cheese
½ cup freshly grated Parmesan cheese
1 egg, beaten
2 tablespoons chopped parsley

Combine cheeses in a small bowl; stir in egg and parsley, blending well. Chill until ready to fill ravioli.

Homemade Tomato Sauce
Makes about 5 cups

1 large onion, chopped (1 cup)
1 clove of garlic, minced
¼ cup olive oil or vegetable oil
1 can (2 pounds, 3 ounces) Italian tomatoes
1 can (6 ounces) tomato paste
2 teaspoons leaf basil, crumbled
1 teaspoon salt
    Dash of sugar
1 cup water

1 Sauté onion and garlic in oil until soft in a large saucepan; stir in tomatoes, tomato paste, basil, salt, sugar and water.

2 Heat to bubbling; reduce heat; simmer, uncovered, stirring frequently, 45 minutes, or until sauce has thickened.

Lasagna Roll-Ups
Bake at 375° for 30 minutes. Makes 6 to 8 servings

1 broiler-fryer (about 2½ pound)
1½ cups water
1 small onion, peeled and sliced
1 teaspoon salt
¼ teaspoon pepper
1 envelope spaghetti sauce mix
1 can (1 pound, 12 ounces) tomato purée
    Dash of sugar
2 tablespoons butter or margarine
1 package (10 ounces) frozen chopped spinach, thawed
¼ teaspoon ground nutmeg
1 pound fluted-edge lasagna noodles
1 package (6 ounces) sliced mozzarella cheese

1 Cook chicken with water, onion, salt and pepper about 40 minutes, or until tender, in a large saucepan.

2 While chicken cooks, combine spaghetti sauce mix, tomato purée, sugar and butter or margarine in a medium-size saucepan. Heat to boiling; reduce heat; cover. Simmer 30 minutes.

3 Remove chicken from broth; cool; reserve broth. Skin chicken; remove from bones, cut meat into small pieces.

4 For filling: Combine ½ cup of the reserved broth with half of the chicken and half of the spinach in an electric blender container. Whirl until smooth, about 1 minute. Place mixture in medium-size bowl, scraping sides of blender container with rubber spatula. Repeat with remaining chicken, spinach and ½ cup broth; add to mixture in bowl; add nutmeg, blending well. (If you do not have a blender, chop chicken and spinach as fine as possible, then stir in enough chicken broth to make a smooth paste.)

5 Cook lasagna noodles in a kettle, following label directions; drain; cool in a large bowl of cold water.

6 To make roll-ups: Remove lasagna noodles, one at a time, from cold water and pat dry with paper toweling. Spread with scant ¼ cup chicken mixture; roll up, jelly-roll fashion. Repeat with remaining noodles.

7 Pour 2 cups of the prepared tomato sauce in the bottom of a shallow 12-cup baking dish. Arrange roll-ups on sauce, making two layers,

1420

Fresh from the oven, brown and bubbling Criss-Cross Lasagna. For the topping, two Italian cheeses—Mozzarella cut in geometric shapes, grated Parmesan.

Lasagna Roll-Ups, not a classic recipe but a superb one.

1421

if necessary. Spoon remaining sauce over roll-ups.

8 Bake in moderate oven (357°) 20 minutes. Cut mozzarella cheese in lengthwise strips and arrange on roll-ups. Bake 10 minutes longer, or until cheese is melted and sauce is bubbly-hot.

Criss-Cross Lasagna
Bake at 350° for 30 minutes. Makes 8 servings

½ *pound sweet or hot Italian sausages*
½ *pound meat-loaf mixture (beef and pork)*
1 *medium-size onion, chopped (½ cup)*
1 *clove garlic, minced*

PASTA AND RICE

1 can (about 2 pounds) Italian tomatoes
1 envelope spaghetti-sauce mix
¼ teaspoon leaf oregano, crumbled
¼ teaspoon ground nutmeg
1 pound lasagna noodles
1 tablespoon olive oil
2 eggs
2 cups (1 pound) ricotta cheese
2 packages (8 ounces each) sliced mozzarella or pizza cheese
½ cup grated Parmesan cheese

1 Squeeze sausages from casings; mix meat lightly with meat-loaf mixture. Shape into a large patty in a frying pan; brown 5 minutes on each side, then break up into chunks; push to one side.
2 Stir in onion and garlic; sauté just until soft. Stir in tomatoes, spaghetti-sauce mix, oregano and nutmeg; simmer, stirring several times, 30 minutes, or until slightly thickened.
3 While sauce cooks, slide lasagna noodles, one at a time so as not to break, into a kettle of boiling salted water. Add olive oil; cook, following label directions. (Oil keeps noodles from sticking.) Cook, stirring often, 15 minutes, or just until tender. Drain; cover with cold water.
4 Beat eggs slightly; blend in cottage cheese.
5 Line bottom of a lightly oiled baking dish, 13x9x2, with a single layer of drained noodles. (Lift each strip separately from water and hold over kettle to drain.) Cover with a third each of cottage-cheese mixture, meat sauce and mozzarella or pizza and Parmesan cheeses. Repeat to make two more layers of each.
6 Bake in moderate oven (350°) 30 minutes,

or until bubbly-hot. Garnish with a ripe-olive "flower" and parsley, if you wish. (To make olive "flower," cut a pitted ripe olive lengthwise into sixths; arrange, petal fashion, around a whole ripe olive.)

Meaty Lasagna Bake
Bake at 425° for 25 minutes. Makes 12 servings

2 packages (1 pound, 8 ounces each) lasagna dinner
2 packages (10 ounces each) frozen chopped spinach
1 pound ground beef or meat-loaf mixture (beef and pork)
2 cups (1-pound carton) cream-style cottage cheese
1 egg
2 teaspoons Italian seasoning
½ teaspoon salt

1 Cook noodles from packages of lasagna dinner, following label directions; drain.
2 Cook spinach, following label directions; drain.
3 Shape ground beef or meat-loaf mixture into a patty in a frying pan; brown 5 minutes on each side, then break up into chunks. Stir in sauce from lasagna dinner.
4 Mix cottage cheese with egg, Italian seasoning and salt; stir in spinach.
5 Set aside 6 noodles. Layer half of remaining noodles, cheese mixture, meat sauce and grated cheese (from packages) into a greased baking dish, 13x9x2. Repeat layers.

Meaty Lasagna Bake is a speedy one-dish dinner made of lasagna mix, meat-loaf mixture and frozen spinach.

6 Roll up saved noodles, jelly-roll fashion; slice in half and press, cut sides down, into sauce.
7 Bake in hot oven (425°) 25 minutes, or until bubbly-hot.

Always a crowd-pleaser: Manicotti alla Bolognese.

Manicotti alla Veneziana

Three kinds of cheese blend in this meatless version of an Italian favorite.
Bake at 350° for 1 hour. Makes 8 servings

1 package (12 ounces) manicotti noodles
2 cups (1 pound) cream-style cottage cheese
1 package (8 ounces) cream cheese
2 packages (10 ounces each) frozen chopped spinach, thawed and drained
2 eggs
2 teaspoons salt
1 teaspoon Italian seasoning
Dash of pepper
6 tablespoons (¾ stick) butter or margarine
6 tablespoons all-purpose flour
1 teaspoon dry mustard
4 cups milk
1 pound Cheddar cheese, grated (4 cups)

1 Cook manicotti noodles, a few at a time, in a large amount of boiling salted water, following label directions; lift out carefully with a slotted spoon so as not to break them; place in cold water until ready to fill.
2 Mix cottage and cream cheeses, one package of the spinach, eggs, 1 teaspoon of the salt, Italian seasoning and pepper until well blended in a medium-size bowl. Place remaining package of spinach in a small bowl and set aside for Step 4.
3 Melt butter or margarine in a medium-size saucepan; stir in flour, remaining 1 teaspoon salt and mustard; cook, stirring constantly, just until bubbly. Stir in milk; continue cooking and stirring until sauce thickens and boils 1 minute; remove from heat. Stir in grated cheese until melted.
4 Blend 1 cup of the sauce into spinach in small bowl; spoon into a shallow baking dish, 13x9x2, to make a layer.
5 Lift manicotti noodles, one at a time, from water; drain well. Fill with cottage-cheese mixture, using a long-handle spoon; place in rows in a single layer over spinach mixture in dish. Spoon remaining cheese sauce over and around noodles.
6 Bake in moderate oven (350°) 1 hour, or until bubbly-hot.

Manicotti alla Bolognese
Makes 6 to 8 servings

1 package (8 ounces) manicotti noodles
1 pound meat-loaf mixture
1 large onion, chopped (1 cup)
1 clove of garlic, minced
1 cup fresh bread crumbs (2 slices)
1 egg, beaten
½ cup chopped parsley
1 teaspoon leaf basil, crumbled
1 teaspoon salt
Dash of pepper
CHEDDAR CHEESE SAUCE (recipe follows)

1 Cook manicotti noodles, a few at a time, following label directions; lift out carefully with a slotted spoon; place in a large bowl of cold water until ready to use.
2 Shape meat-loaf mixture into a large patty in a large skillet; brown 5 minutes on each side, then break up into small pieces; remove with a slotted spoon to a medium-size bowl.
3 Sauté onion and garlic until soft in drippings in skillet. Add to cooked meat with bread crumbs, egg, parsley, basil, salt and pepper, mixing until well blended.
4 Lift manicotti noodles from water, one at a time; drain well. Fill each with part of the meat mixture, using a long-handled spoon.
5 Pour half the hot CHEDDAR CHEESE SAUCE into the bottom of a shallow 12-cup flameproof dish. Place filled manicotti over cheese sauce. Top with remaining sauce.
6 Broil, 4 inches from heat, 5 minutes, or until golden and bubbly.
Note—MANICOTTI ALLA BOLOGNESE can be made early in the day and refrigerated. About 45 minutes before serving time, warm in moderate oven (350°) 30 minutes, then place under broiler until golden and bubbly.

1423

Cheddar Cheese Sauce
Makes about 2½ cups

4 tablespoons (½ stick) butter or margarine
¼ cup sifted all-purpose flour

¼ teaspoon salt
· Dash of pepper
2½ cups milk
1 teaspoon Worcestershire sauce
½ pound Cheddar cheese, shredded (2 cups)

1 Melt butter or margarine in a medium-size saucepan. Blend in flour, salt and pepper; cook, stirring constantly, just until bubbly.
2 Stir in milk; continue cooking and stirring until sauce thickens and bubbles 1 minute. Stir in cheese and Worcestershire sauce until cheese is melted.

Homemade Egg Noodles
Makes about 1 pound uncooked noodles

4 eggs
1 teaspoon salt
2¾ cups sifted all-purpose flour

1 Beat eggs well with salt in a medium-size bowl. Stir in 1 cup of the flour, then mix in enough of the remaining flour to form a stiff dough.
2 Turn out onto a lightly floured pastry cloth or board. Knead, adding a little extra flour to keep dough from sticking, 5 minutes, or until smooth. Shape into a ball; cover with a bowl turned upside down. Let stand on board about 30 minutes. Divide in half.
3 Roll out, half at a time, into a large thin sheet; hang dough on a towel spread over the back of a straight-back chair. (Another idea is to make a rack by placing a long dowel or broom handle over the back of two chairs.) Let dough hang about 30 minutes, or until dry but still workable.
4 Roll up each sheet, jelly-roll fashion; cut into ¼-inch-wide slices. Separate slices, then unroll strips; spread out on board. Let stand to dry, turning several times, about 30 minutes. Cut strips in half, if you wish. Cook, following your favorite recipe.

Saucy Noodle Crown
Mold cooked noodles into a custard-rich ring, fill with green beans and serve with cold cuts or steamed frankfurters.
Bake at 350° for 30 minutes. Makes 6 servings

1425

Pasta parade (front, l. to r.): fusilli and sour cream, Fettuccini Verde, Spaghetti with Red Clam Sauce; (rear): Farfalle Leonardo; pizza pan of spaghetti topped with sauce, cheese, cold cuts; Macaroni and Cheese.

½ pound fine noodles
1 small onion, chopped
4 tablespoons (½ stick) butter or margarine
4 tablespoons all-purpose flour
1 can (3 or 4 ounces) sliced mushrooms
¾ cup milk
1 cup grated Cheddar cheese (4 ounces)
1 tablespoon prepared mustard
3 eggs
   GREEN BEANS NAPOLI (recipe follows)

1 Cook noodles, following label directions; drain.
2 Sauté onion in butter or margarine until soft in a medium-size saucepan; stir in flour; cook, stirring constantly, until bubbly. Stir in liquid from mushrooms and milk; continue cooking and stirring until sauce thickens and boils 1 minute. Stir in cheese until melted and mustard; remove from heat.
3 Beat eggs slightly in a large bowl; gradually beat in cheese mixture; fold in cooked noodles and mushrooms. Spoon into a greased 8-cup ring mold. Set mold in a baking pan on oven shelf; pour boiling water into pan to a depth of about an inch.
4 Bake in moderate oven (350°) 30 minutes, or until set; remove from pan of water. Let ring stand several minutes, then loosen around edge and center; invert onto a serving plate. Spoon GREEN BEANS NAPOLI into center.
   GREEN BEANS NAPOLI—Cook 2 packages (9 ounces each) frozen cut green beans, following label directions; drain. Heat 1 can (about 1 pound) stewed tomatoes with 1 teaspoon basil to boiling in a medium-size saucepan. Blend 1 tablespoon cornstarch with 2 tablespoons water until smooth in a cup; stir into hot tomato mixture. Cook, stirring constantly, until sauce thickens and boils 3 minutes; fold in green beans.

Noodles Napoli
Makes 6 servings

1 pound ground beef
½ pound sausage meat
1 medium-size onion, chopped (½ cup)
½ clove garlic, minced
½ pound fine noodles
2 cans (about 1 pound each) tomatoes
½ cup water
1 pimiento, chopped
1½ teaspoons salt
1 cup grated Cheddar cheese (4 ounces)

1 Mix ground beef and sausage meat; shape

into a large patty in a large frying pan; brown 5 minutes on each side, then break up into chunks. Remove and set aside.
2 Pour off all drippings, then measure 3 tablespoonfuls and return to pan; stir in onion and garlic and sauté just until soft. Add uncooked noodles; continue cooking, stirring often, until noodles are toasty-golden.
3 Stir in tomatoes, water, pimiento, salt and browned meat; cover.
4 Simmer, stirring often, 10 minutes; stir in cheese; cover again. Cook 10 minutes longer, or until noodles are tender and cheese is melted.

German Casserole
Bake at 350° for 45 minutes. Makes 4 servings

2 cups (half an 8-ounce package) noodles
1 can (about 1 pound) sauerkraut, drained
1 pound ground beef
1 egg
½ cup soft caraway-rye bread crumbs
¼ cup milk
1 teaspoon salt
⅛ teaspoon pepper
1 tablespoon butter or margarine
1 can (about 1 pound) stewed tomatoes

1 Cook noodles and drain, following label directions; stir in drained sauerkraut.
2 Mix ground beef lightly with egg, bread crumbs, milk, salt and pepper until well blended; shape into 24 balls. Brown in butter or margarine in a large frying pan; stir in tomatoes.
3 Spoon half of the noodle-sauerkraut mixture into an 8-cup baking dish; top with half of the meatball mixture; repeat layers; cover.
4 Bake in moderate oven (350°) 45 minutes, or until bubbly-hot in center.

Noodles Romanoff
One of the most popular of all ways with noodles. Cottage and Parmesan cheeses blend with sour cream for the rich sauce.
Bake at 350° for 30 minutes. Makes 6 servings

½ pound regular noodles
1 cup (8 ounces) cream-style cottage cheese
1 cup dairy sour cream
½ cup grated Parmesan cheese
1 teaspoon grated onion
1 teaspoon Worcestershire sauce

1 Cook noodles in boiling salted water in a kettle, following label directions; drain; return to kettle.

2 Stir in remaining ingredients; spoon into a 6-cup baking dish.

3 Bake in moderate oven (350°) 30 minutes, or until hot. Sprinkle with chopped parsley, if you wish.

Tuna-Noodle Surprise

Crunchy cashew nuts give this popular dish a delightful flavor touch.

Bake at 350° for 35 minutes. Makes 6 servings

½ pound wide noodles
2 cups frozen green peas (from a 2-pound bag)
1 can (10½ ounces) condensed cream of celery soup
1 can (3 or 4 ounces) sliced mushrooms
1 cup milk
Few drops Worcestershire sauce
½ pound unsliced process cheese, cut in small pieces
2 cans (about 7 ounces each) tuna, drained and flaked
1 package (about 3 ounces) salted cashew nuts, chopped coarsely

1 Cook noodles in unsalted water, following label directions; drain; return to kettle; place peas on top to thaw.

2 Heat soup, mushrooms and liquid, milk, Worcestershire sauce and cheese, stirring frequently, until cheese is melted, in medium-size saucepan; stir into noodles and peas; mix well. Gently fold in tuna. Pour into 12-cup casserole; cover.

3 Bake in moderate oven (350°) 30 minutes;

Fettuccini Alfredo
Makes 4 servings

3 cups sifted all-purpose flour
2 teaspoons salt
3 eggs
3 tablespoons olive oil or vegetable oil
¼ cup cold water
Cornstarch
½ cup (1 stick) butter or margarine, cut in small pieces
2 cups freshly grated Parmesan cheese
Freshly ground black pepper

1 Sift flour and salt into a large bowl; make a well in center; add eggs, oil and water. Work liquids into flour with fingers to make a stiff dough.

2 Turn dough out onto a large pastry board. (Do not add additional flour.) Knead 10 minutes, or until dough is as smooth and soft as perfectly kneaded bread dough. Wrap dough in plastic wrap and allow to rest at room temperature 1 hour.

3 Sprinkle pastry board with cornstarch. Roll out dough, a quarter at a time, to a rectangle so thin you can see through the dough.

4 Fold dough into quarters lengthwise. Slice dough across into ¼-inch-wide strips. Unwind strips and allow to dry on clean towels for 1 hour. Repeat with remaining quarters of dough.

5 Heat 6 quarts of water to boiling in a large kettle; add 2 tablespoons salt and 1 tablespoon oil. Cook fettucini 5 minutes, or until they are cooked to the tenderness you like. Drain well and turn out onto a heated serving platter.

6 Add pieces of butter or margarine and toss with fork and spoon until butter melts. Add Parmesan cheese and continue to toss until fettucini are coated and glistening. For that final touch, grind black pepper over the top.

Tortellini

Tiny crescents of noodle dough are filled with a spinach and cheese mixture and baked in a meaty tomato sauce.

Bake at 350° for 30 minutes. Makes 8 servings

1 recipe FETTUCINI ALFREDO (recipe precedes)
1 package (10 ounces) frozen chopped spinach, thawed
1 carton (1 pound) ricotta cheese
   OR: Cream-style cottage cheese
1 teaspoon salt
¼ teaspoon grated nutmeg
1 pound ground beef
2 cans (15 ounces each) special tomato sauce
½ cup dry red wine

1 Roll out FETTUCINI ALFREDO dough, one-quarter at a time, on a pastry board lightly sprinkled with cornstarch, until thin enough to see through the dough.

2 Cut out dough with a 3-inch round cutter. (You will get about 96 rounds.)

3 Press all water out of spinach and drain on paper toweling. Combine spinach, ricotta or cottage cheese, salt and nutmeg in a small bowl. Place ½ teaspoon on each round; fold in half and press edges tightly together to seal and

1427

twist into a crescent shape. Continue until all rounds are filled. (You will have extra filling.)

4 Cook pasta, 24 at a time, in a large kettle of boiling water, to which 2 tablespoons salt and 1 tablespoon vegetable oil have been added, 10 minutes, or just until tender; drain.

5 Press ground beef into a large patty in a large skillet. Brown on one side for 5 minutes; turn and brown 5 minutes on second side. Drain off excess fat and chop into tiny pieces. Stir in tomato sauce and wine. Simmer 10 minutes.

6 Layer pasta, remaining filling and tomato mixture in a 13x9x2-inch baking dish.

7 Bake in moderate oven (350°) 30 minutes, or until casserole is bubbly-hot.

Fettuccini Verde
(Green Noodles)
Makes 4 servings

½ pound green noodles
½ cup (1 stick) butter or margarine
1 can (3 or 4 ounces) sliced mushrooms, drained
1 whole pimiento, drained and chopped
½ cup freshly grated Parmesan cheese
Freshly grated black pepper

1 Cook noodles in a kettle, following label directions; drain; place on large heated serving platter.

2 While noodles cook, melt butter or margarine in small saucepan; add mushrooms and pimiento, cooking and stirring until piping-hot.

3 Pour butter mixture over noodles; add grated cheese and pepper; toss lightly until noodles are evenly coated. Serve immediately.

Linguine alla Maria Teresa
(Noodle and Ham Casserole
Bake at 400° for 20 minutes. Makes 8 servings

1 pound linguine or spaghetti
4 cups diced cooked ham
   OR: 1 can (1 pound) ham, diced
6 tablespoons (¾ stick) butter or margarine
1 can (3 or 4 ounces) sliced or chopped mushrooms
4 tablespoons all-purpose flour
1 teaspoon salt
1 tall can (14½ ounces) evaporated milk
1 envelope instant chicken broth
   OR: 1 teaspoon granulated chicken bouillon
1⅓ cups water
½ cup grated Romano cheese
1 sweet red pepper
1 green pepper
1 tablespoon butter or margarine (for peppers)
1 cup packaged croutons

1 Cook linguine in a kettle, following label directions; drain; return to kettle.

2 While linguine cook, brown ham slightly in the 6 tablespoons butter or margarine in a large saucepan; remove with slotted spoon to a small bowl.

3 Drain mushroom liquid into a cup; reserve mushrooms for Step 4. Blend flour and salt into drippings in saucepan; cook, stirring constantly, just until bubbly. Stir in mushroom liquid, milk, chicken broth and water. Continue cooking and stirring until sauce thickens and bubbles 1 minute.

4 Add 2 cups of the sauce and reserved mushrooms to drained linguine; toss to mix. Spoon into a shallow 10-cup baking dish, pressing linguine up sides of dish to leave a hollow in center. Add reserved ham to remaining sauce, blending well. Spoon into hollow in pasta. Sprinkle with Romano cheese.

1428

Unusual way to trim Fettuccini Verde—with butter-broiled mushroom buttons and sweet red pepper squares.

5 Bake in hot oven (400°) 20 minutes, or until bubbly.
6 Meanwhile, halve, seed and slice peppers; sauté in the 1 tablespoon butter or margarine until soft in a small skillet; keep warm.
7 Sprinkle croutons around edge of casserole and mound sautéed peppers in the center.

Farfalle Leonardo

Tiny egg-noodle bows are tossed with a quick, yet rich, tomato sauce for super family eating.
Makes 4 servings

1 pound bulk sausage
1 large onion, chopped (1 cup)
1 clove of garlic, minced
1 can (1 pound) tomatoes
1 teaspoon leaf oregano, crumbled
1 teaspoon leaf basil, crumbled
1 teaspoon salt
⅛ teaspoon pepper
½ pound farfalle
½ cup grated Parmesan cheese

1 Flatten sausage meat into a large patty in a large skillet. Brown on one side; turn and brown on second side. Remove sausage from skillet and crumble onto paper towels.
2 Drain off all but 2 tablespoons of fat in skillet. Sauté onion and garlic in skillet until soft. Drain tomatoes; reserve liquid. Brown tomatoes in same skillet for 5 minutes. (This is an Italian cooking trick for a tomato sauce with special flavor.)
3 Return crumbled sausage to skillet with liquid from canned tomatoes, oregano, basil, salt and pepper. Simmer, stirring occasionally, 30 minutes.
4 Cook farfalle, following label directions, until done as you like pasta. Drain and place on large heated serving platter. Spoon sauce over and top with Parmesan cheese. Mix lightly at the table and serve at once.

Potato Gnocchi

Dumplings, Northern Italian style, tender and cheesy.
Bake at 400° for 15 minutes. Makes 8 servings

2 pounds potatoes, pared
2 eggs, beaten
1 teaspoon salt
3 cups sifted all-purpose flour
1 can (10½ ounces) condensed chicken broth
8 cups water
½ cup (1 stick) butter or margarine, melted
1 cup grated Parmesan cheese

1 Cook potatoes in boiling salted water until tender in a large saucepan; drain and toss over very low heat 2 minutes to dry potatoes.
2 Mash potatoes until smooth in a large bowl; beat in eggs and salt. Blend in flour to make a soft dough. Cover bowl and chill at least 1 hour.
3 Heat chicken broth and water to boiling in a large kettle. Drop dough by teaspoonfuls, a few at a time, into boiling liquid and simmer 5 minutes, or until slightly puffed. Remove with a slotted spoon to a shallow baking dish.
4 Drizzle with melted butter or margarine and sprinkle with cheese.
5 Bake in hot oven (400°) 15 minutes, or until puffy and golden. Serve at once.

Creamy Macaroni and Cheese

Bake at 350° for 30 minutes. Makes 6 servings

½ pound elbow macaroni
1 small onion, grated
2 tablespoons butter or margarine
2 tablespoons instant-type flour
1 teaspoon Worcestershire sauce
½ teaspoon salt
2½ cups milk
1 package (8 ounces) process sharp Cheddar cheese, grated
1 cup buttered bread crumbs

1 Stir macaroni into a big pan of boiling salted water; cook, stirring often, just until tender; drain.
2 Spoon macaroni into an 8-cup baking dish. Make sauce: Blend onion, butter or margarine, flour, seasonings, milk and cheese in a saucepan. Cook, stirring constantly, until sauce thickens and boils 1 minute. Pour over macaroni, then mix in.
3 Sprinkle buttered bread crumbs in a ring on top. (To fix, crumble 2 slices bread; toss with 1 tablespoon melted butter or margarine.) Bake in moderate oven (350°) 30 minutes, or until center is bubbly-hot and crumbs are toasty-golden.

1429

Blue and Gold Macaroni Bake

Reliable as ever and twice as satisfying made with both blue cheese and Cheddar.
Bake at 350° for 30 minutes. Makes 6 servings

½ pound elbow macaroni
4 tablespoons (½ stick) butter or margarine
¼ cup sifted all-purpose flour
1 small onion, grated
1 tablespoon Worcestershire sauce
2 teaspoons dry mustard

1 teaspoon salt
2½ cups milk
1 pound Cheddar cheese, shredded (4 cups)
¼ cup crumbled blue cheese
1 cup soft white-bread crumbs (2 slices)

1 Cook macaroni, following label directions; drain; spoon into an 8-cup baking dish.
2 Melt butter or margarine in a medium-size saucepan; stir in flour, onion, Worcestershire sauce, mustard and salt; cook, stirring constantly, just until bubbly.
3 Stir in milk; continue cooking and stirring until sauce thickens and boils 1 minute; stir in Cheddar and blue cheeses until melted.
4 Pour over macaroni; stir lightly to mix. Sprinkle bread crumbs over top.
5 Bake in moderate oven (350°) 30 minutes, or until bubbly and golden.

Pasta e Fagioli
A hearty Italian macaroni dish, traditionally served in soup bowls.
Makes 6 generous servings

1 large onion, chopped (1 cup)
1 small clove of garlic, minced
2 tablespoons vegetable oil
2 envelopes instant chicken bouillon
    OR: 2 chicken-bouillon cubes
4 cups water
½ pound macaroni shells
4 cups diced cooked pork
1 can (about 1 pound) tomatoes
1 can (about 1 pound) red kidney beans
1 bay leaf
1 teaspoon salt
½ teaspoon leaf oregano, crumbled
¼ teaspoon pepper
¼ cup grated Parmesan cheese
1 tablespoon chopped parsley

1430

1 Sauté onion and garlic in salad oil just until softened in large kettle or Dutch oven. Add chicken bouillon or cubes and water; cover; heat to boiling. Stir in macaroni shells; cook 10 minutes, or until almost tender.
2 Stir in remaining ingredients, except cheese and parsley. Heat to boiling, stirring often. Cook 10 minutes, or until macaroni is tender; remove bay leaf.
3 Ladle into heated soup bowls or plates; sprinkle cheese and parsley over.

SOME PASTA SAUCES

Meat Ball Sauce
The most popular of all spaghetti toppers.
Makes 5 cups

1 pound ground beef
1 cup soft bread crumbs (2 slices)
2 cans (about 10 ounces each) spaghetti sauce with mushrooms
2 tablespoons butter or margarine
1 can (8 ounces) tomato sauce

1 Mix ground beef with bread crumbs and ½ cup of the spaghetti sauce in a medium-size bowl; shape into 24 small balls.
2 Brown in butter or margarine in a large frying pan; stir in remaining spaghetti and tomato sauces. Simmer 15 minutes to blend flavors. Spoon over hot cooked spaghetti.

Speedy Sausage Sauce
Makes 3 cups

½ pound sweet Italian sausages
1 jar (24 ounces) meatless spaghetti sauce
    Dash of sugar

1 Cut sausages into ½-inch slices. Cook slowly until well done in a medium-size skillet; drain off fat.
2 Add spaghetti sauce and sugar to sausage; heat to bubbling; reduce heat. Simmer 5 minutes to blend flavors. Serve sauce over spaghettini, fusilli, or vermicelli.

Taormina Sauce
Delicate chicken livers make this unusual sauce.
Makes 5 cups

½ pound chicken livers, halved
3 tablespoons olive oil
1 large onion, chopped (1 cup)
1 envelope spaghetti sauce mix without tomato
1 can (about 1 pound) stewed tomatoes
¼ cup water

1 Sauté livers slowly in olive oil in a medium-size saucepan just until they lose their pink color; remove.
2 Sauté onion until soft in drippings in same pan; stir in remaining ingredients; simmer 15 minutes. Add livers; heat just until hot. Spoon over hot cooked spaghetti.

Parsley-Basil-Clam Sauce
It's garlicky, but clam fans say "just right."
Makes 3 cups

2 cloves garlic, crushed
3 tablespoons butter or margarine
3 tablespoons olive oil
2 cans (about 7 ounces each) minced clams
½ cup chopped parsley
½ cup chopped fresh basil leaves
¼ teaspoon freshly ground pepper

1 Sauté garlic in butter or margarine and olive oil 3 minutes, or until soft in a medium-size saucepan.
2 Stir in clams and liquid, parsley, basil and pepper; simmer 5 minutes. Spoon over hot cooked spaghetti.

Quick Trick: rolled-up leftover roast with spaghetti.

Mushroom Spaghetti Sauce
For 1 pound spaghetti or linguine. Makes 6 servings

6 tablespoons (¾ stick) butter or margarine
4 medium onions, thinly sliced
2 pounds mushrooms
  Salt
  Freshly ground pepper
⅛ teaspoon ground nutmeg
1 cup heavy cream
  Freshly grated Parmesan cheese

1 Melt 3 tablespoons of the butter or margarine in a large heavy skillet. Sauté onions, stirring frequently, over medium heat 5 minutes, or until golden. Lower the heat to lowest possible. Cover the skillet and cook, stirring occasionally, for about 30 minutes. The onions must be very soft, but not browned.
2 While the onions are cooking, wash and drain the mushrooms. Cut off the tip of the stem and slice the mushrooms thinly lengthwise, including the stem. Heat the remaining butter or margarine in another skillet. Sauté the mushrooms in it, stirring frequently, over medium heat until soft.
3 Add the mushrooms to the onions. Season with salt and pepper to taste; stir in the nutmeg. Mix well. Keep the sauce hot, over lowest possible heat, while the spaghetti is cooking.
4 Five minutes before serving, add the cream to the sauce. Stir well and heat through. Do not boil or the sauce will curdle.
5 Drain spaghetti and place in a serving dish.

Pour sauce over spaghetti; toss thoroughly. Serve immediately, with grated Parmesan cheese on the side.

6 JIFFY PASTA SAUCES

Start with an envelope spaghetti-sauce mix:
  BITSY BURGER SAUCE—Mix ½ pound ground beef; 1 small onion, chopped (¼ cup); ½ teaspoon salt; and ½ teaspoon crumbled leaf marjoram in a medium-size bowl. Shape into a patty in a medium-size frying pan. Brown 5 minutes on each side, then break up into large chunks. Prepare 1 envelope spaghetti-sauce mix *without* tomato, following label directions; stir in 1 teaspoon sugar. Pour over meat; heat until bubbly. Makes about 3 cups.
  BONUS MEAT SAUCE—Prepare 1 envelope spaghetti-sauce mix *with* tomato, following label directions; stir in 1 cup diced cooked lamb or veal, ½ cup chopped celery, 1 teaspoon sugar and ½ teaspoon crumbled leaf rosemary. Simmer 10 minutes to blend flavors. Makes about 3 cups.

1431

Start with canned spaghetti sauce with mushrooms:
  MARINARA SAUCE—Stir 1 can (about 8 ounces) minced clams and liquid, 2 tablespoons chopped parsley, 1 tablespoon lemon juice and 2 teaspoons sugar into 1 can (about 1 pound) spaghetti sauce with mushrooms in a medium-size saucepan. Heat just until bubbly. Makes about 2 cups.
  CHEESE 'N' MUSHROOM SAUCE—Stir ¾ cup chopped celery, 1 teaspoon prepared mustard and 1 teaspoon sugar into 1 can (about 1 pound) spaghetti sauce with mushrooms in a

medium-size saucepan; heat until bubbly. Dice 1 package (8 ounces) mozzarella cheese; stir into sauce. Spoon over cooked spaghetti before cheese melts. Makes 2¼ cups.

Start with canned condensed tomato soup:

WIENER-RING SAUCE—Combine 1 cup sliced frankfurters (about 2), 1 can (3 or 4 ounces) chopped mushrooms and liquid, 1 teaspoon sugar, 1 teaspoon mixed Italian herbs, ¼ cup water and 1 can (10¾ ounces) condensed tomato soup in a medium-size saucepan; simmer 10 minutes. Makes 2½ cups.

FRIDAY HERB SAUCE —Combine 1 package (10 ounces) frozen fillet of flounder, 2 teaspoons sugar, 1 teaspoon crumbled leaf basil, 1 teaspoon chopped chives and 2 cans (10¾ ounces each) condensed tomato soup in a large saucepan; simmer 5 minutes. Flake fish into large pieces; simmer 5 minutes longer. Makes 4 cups.

What boiled rice should look like—fluffy, not gummy.

ALL ABOUT RICE

1432

THE OLD-TIME FAVORITES:

These are the leaders of more than a dozen varieties available for your eating pleasure.

White Rice—Dubbed "regular" because it is the most familiar and popular. Hull, bran and polishings have been removed, leaving a snow-white grain. Size regulates price, with short or medium grain as the thriftiest. It cooks moist and tender, and is an ideal choice for casseroles, puddings and croquettes. Long-grain rice, at a few pennies more a pound, cooks

fluffier and flakier and is preferred for serving as a vegetable or a base for curry or Chinese-style dishes. Most white rice is enriched, but let the label be your guide.

Processed White Rice—The description of "parboiled" or "converted" on its package simply means that the grains have been partly cooked before milling, with special care taken to protect the important vitamins and minerals in the outer layer. This rice is long-grain with a light golden color and cooks the same as regular rice.

Precooked White Rice—Busy homemakers call it "instant" because it needs only the briefest cooking. It is milled from special long-grain rice, is enriched and comes both plain and seasoned for making instant Spanish rice.

Brown Rice—This is whole-grain rice with only the outer hull removed. Cooking time is longer than for regular white rice, and its nutlike flavor makes it a favorite for serving with meat, game or as a vegetable.

Wild Rice—This is not a true rice but the seed of a water grass native to some of our northern states. Supply is limited and the gathering, done from small boats, is slow—the reasons for its seemingly high price. When cooked, these long slender gray-brown grains have a sweet nutlike flavor, specially favored with game. Wild rice is available plain or mixed with long-grain white rice or precooked and packaged in cans.

THE JET-AGE WINNERS:

Talk about convenience! Rice is 'way out front with specialties to spark many a plain meal. Consider these choices:

Seasoned Rice—Seasonings are mixed with long-grain rice before packaging in long slim bags. Take your pick of beef, chicken, chili, cheese, curry, herb, pilaf and yellow rice.

Specialties—Name your kind and it's probably available. In the grocery department you'll find Chinese fried rice in little cardboard buckets . . . Spanish rice in cans, also in packages that needs only the addition of tomatoes to turn it into a family-size meal in minutes . . . packaged rice mixed with thin pasta sticks and seasoned with chicken, cheese and tomato . . . rice pudding in cans, ready to eat, and in boxes for a quick do-it-yourself dessert. In some specialty departments is a new rice-curry dinner complete with the rice, curry sauce, peanuts and chutney. And in the frozen-food cabinet frozen fried rice is heading for stardom.

EVERY PENNY COUNTS!

Rice is one of your biggest budget boosters. And since there's no waste in fixing, no loss in cooking, you get exactly what you pay for. Buy it in packages from a one-cup measure for live-aloners to a 2- to 5-pound box or bag for rice-eating families. And remember, the larger the box, the lower the cost per serving. A few serving ideas:

• Mix varieties—white with brown rice or brown with wild rice for a new flavor twist as well as for smart "stretching."

• Star rice as the vegetable of the meal or use it as a base for creamed fish, eggs or meat.

• Combine rice with cut-up meat or chicken from yesterday's roast, or with eggs, cheese or canned fish for a casserole to pull you through a before-payday squeeze.

• Season rice with a buttery sauce, exotic spices or herbs, chopped nuts, snips of chives or parsley, or flaked coconut to dress your buffet or party table.

• Fold sweetened whipped cream, toasted almonds and cut-up fruits—maraschino cherries, pineapple, oranges, peaches, bananas—into cooked rice for a quick-fix creamy-good dessert.

• Toss cooked rice with diced vegetables, chicken or seafood and salad dressing for a main-dish luncheon or supper salad.

• Add rice to your favorite soup for extra heartiness or to make it go just a bit further.

• Serve rice plain with milk or cream for breakfast, or when someone is ill. Its mild flavor and easy digestibility make it an all-around family food, a perfect choice for all ages.

How Much Rice?

A good general rule to remember is that rice swells from three to four times its measure when cooked. Here is a handy chart to use for quick reference.

1 Cup Uncooked	Measure After Cooking	Servings*
Regular white rice	3 cups	3 to 4
Long-grain white rice	4 cups	4 to 6
Processed white rice	4 cups	4 to 6
Precooked white rice	2 cups	2 to 3
Brown rice	4 cups	4 to 6
Wild rice	4 cups	4 to 6

*Based on ⅔ to 1 cup for each serving

How to Cook Rice:

Follow label directions, or steam or bake it these no-fuss, no-watch ways and it will come out plump, tender and fluffy every time. The two easy secrets: Accurate measuring and a snug cover for your cooking pot. To make four cups cooked rice, you will need:

> 2½ cups water
> 1 tablespoon butter or margarine
> 1 teaspoon salt
> 1 cup uncooked long-grain or processed white rice

Steam It This Way: Measure the 2½ cups water, butter or margarine and salt into the top of a double boiler; heat to boiling over direct heat, then stir in the rice; cover. Place top of double boiler over bottom half filled with boiling water; turn heat to medium, and cook 45 minutes, or until water is absorbed completely and rice is fluffy-dry and tender. Toss lightly with a fork to fluff up, season as you wish, and serve.

Bake It This Way: Combine rice, salt and butter or margarine in a 4- to 6-cup baking dish. Pour in 2½ cups *boiling* water; stir well; cover. Bake in moderate oven (350°) 1 hour, or until water is absorbed and rice is tender. Fluff up with a fork.

QUICK Q AND A ON RICE

Q. *Should rice be washed before it's cooked?*

A. No. Washing cleanly packaged rice just wastes valuable minerals and vitamins. This old theory probably dates back to the time when rice was dusted with talcum powder that needed to be washed off before cooking.

Q. *Should rice be rinsed after cooking?*

A. The answer is the same as for washing before cooking. When properly cooked, rice shouldn't need even to be drained.

Q. *Can cooked rice be reheated?*

A. Yes, and so simply. Just pour enough water into a saucepan to cover the bottom; spoon in rice, and steam about 5 minutes, or until water is absorbed and rice is fluffy again.

Q. *Can cooked dishes be frozen?*

A. They can, but grains tend to harden somewhat. In preparing casserole dishes for freezing, we have found best results with this method: Cook rice as directed, then stir in ¼ cup extra liquid—milk, broth or tomato juice—for each 1 cup of cooked rice before mixing with other ingredients. Let the rice stand in its cooker until this liquid is absorbed, then mix. When the casserole is reheated, this extra liquid keeps the rice soft and moist.

Mexican Rice Ring
Bake at 350° for 30 minutes. Makes 12 servings

6 cups cooked rice
½ pound Monterey Jack cheese, shredded
  OR: ½ pound Cheddar cheese, shredded
1 can (4 ounces) peeled green chili peppers, chopped
2 teaspoons salt
1 teaspoon pepper
2 cups (16-ounce carton) dairy sour cream
1 pimiento, cut in thin strips

1 Combine rice with cheese, chili peppers, salt and pepper in a large bowl; toss lightly to mix. Fold in sour cream. Spoon into an 8-cup ring mold, packing mixture down lightly with back of spoon.
2 Bake in moderate oven (350°) 30 minutes, or until set.
3 Cool in mold on a wire rack 5 minutes. Loosen around edge and center ring with a knife; cover with a serving plate. Turn upside down; gently lift off mold.
4 Place pimiento strips over top of ring. Fill center with celery leaves and tomato wedges, and frame base with shredded lettuce, if you wish.

1434

Rice Mingle
Cook brown and white rices together for this inviting curry partner.
Makes 4 servings

½ cup uncooked brown rice
1 teaspoon salt
3 cups boiling water
½ cup uncooked regular rice
1 pimiento, diced
¼ cup chopped pecans or pistachio nuts

1 Stir brown rice and salt into boiling water in

large heavy saucepan; cover; simmer 20 minutes.
2 Stir in regular rice; cover again; simmer, stirring once or twice with a fork, 15 to 20 minutes longer, or until rices are tender and water is absorbed.
3 Stir in pimiento and nuts; heat, shaking pan gently, 1 to 2 minutes to dry and fluff rice.

Spicy Pilaf
Chili powder and mace gives this fix-easy rice a mild let's-have-some-more flavor.
Makes 6 servings

1 cup uncooked regular rice
1 medium-size onion, chopped (1 cup)
½ teaspoon ground mace
½ teaspoon chili powder
3 tablespoons vegetable oil
2 envelopes instant chicken broth
  OR: 2 chicken-bouillon cubes
½ teaspoon salt
2¼ cups water

1 Combine rice with the onion, mace, chili powder and vegetable oil in the top of a medium-size double boiler; sauté stirring constantly, over direct heat, just until rice is toasty-golden.
2 Stir in instant chicken broth or bouillon cubes, salt and water; heat to boiling, stirring constantly and crushing cubes, if using, with a spoon. Set double-boiler top over simmering water; cover.
3 Cook 30 minutes, or until liquid is absorbed and rice is tender. Stir lightly with a fork to fluff up rice before serving.
Note—If rice must stand awhile, keep it in its double-boiler cooker over hot water.

Skillet Pilaf
Toast the rice first, then steam with seasonings. Delicious with lamb.
Makes 6 servings

1 cup uncooked regular rice
3 tablespoons peanut oil or vegetable oil
¼ cup chopped green onions
1 can (3 or 4 ounces) chopped mushrooms
3 tablespoons soy sauce
2 cups hot water

1 Sauté rice, stirring often, in peanut oil or vegetable oil until toasty-brown in a large frying pan; stir in green onions; cook 2 minutes longer.
2 Stir in remaining ingredients; cover. Simmer 20 minutes, or unti rice is tender and liquid is absorbed.

Pimiento-striped Mexican Rice Ring, laced with chili peppers, sour cream and mellow Monterey Jack cheese.

PASTA AND RICE

Brown Rice Pilaf
Easy but fancy—and so good with chicken or lamb.
Makes 6 servings

1 cup uncooked brown rice
3 tablespoons vegetable oil
1 large onion, chopped (1 cup)
2 envelopes instant beef broth
1 teaspoon salt
½ teaspoon ground cumin
⅛ teaspoon pepper
3 cups water

1 Sauté rice, stirring constantly, in vegetable oil until toasted in a large frying pan; remove and set aside. Stir onion into pan; sauté until soft.
2 Stir in remaining ingredients; heat to boiling; return rice; cover.
3 Simmer 1 hour and 15 minutes, or until rice is tender and liquid is absorbed. Fluff rice with a fork before serving.

Herbed Pilaf
Pan-toasted rice and bulgur wheat make this delectable go-with for curried turkey.
Makes 8 servings

1 cup uncooked long-grain rice
¼ cup peanut oil or vegetable oil
1 large onion, chopped (1 cup)
1 cup chopped celery
4 envelopes instant chicken broth
  OR: 4 chicken-bouillon cubes

1 teaspoon leaf rosemary, crumbled
4 cups water
1 cup bulgur wheat or wheat pilaf (from a 1-pound package)

1 Sauté rice, stirring constantly, in peanut oil or vegetable oil until toasty-golden in a large frying pan; remove with a slotted spoon and set aside. Stir onion and celery into drippings in pan; sauté just until soft.
2 Stir in chicken broth or bouillon cubes, rosemary and water; heat to boiling, crushing cubes, if using, with a spoon. Stir in bulgur wheat and browned rice; cover.
3 Simmer, stirring once or twice, 1 hour, or until liquid is absorbed and wheat and rice are fluffy-tender.

Louisiana Boiled Rice
Makes 8 servings

3 quarts water
2 tablespoons butter or margarine
1 tablespoon salt
2 cups uncooked regular rice

1 Heat water, butter or margarine and salt to boiling in a large heavy saucepan. Stir in rice and heat to boiling.
2 Boil rice 15 minutes, or until tender. Drain rice in a large strainer. Pack into a buttered 8-cup bowl; cover bowl with foil.
3 Keep rice warm in a very low oven (250°) until ready to serve.

Tibetan Rice
It cooks fluffy-light without watching and has an exotic Far Eastern flavor.
Makes 4 servings

¾ cup uncooked regular rice
2 tablespoons vegetable oil
½ teaspoon turmeric
½ teaspoon curry powder
½ teaspoon salt
¼ cup seedless raisins
  Water
1 can (10½ ounces) condensed chicken broth
  OR: 2 chicken-bouillon cubes

1 Stir rice into vegetable oil in top of medium-size double boiler; heat over direct heat, stirring constantly, until rice is well coated.
2 Blend in turmeric, curry powder and salt; stir in raisins. Add enough water to broth to make 1½ cups (or use bouillon cubes dissolved in 1½ cups boiling water); stir into rice mixture.
3 Cover; cook over simmering water, 1 hour,

The "bread of the Orient"—a bowl of boiled rice.

or until rice is fluffed and tender and liquid is absorbed.

Pimiento Rice
Bake at 375° about 40 minutes. Makes 6 servings

1½ cups uncooked regular rice
4 tablespoons (½ stick) butter or margarine
1 can (10¼ ounces) condensed beef bouillon
1½ cups water
1 teaspoon instant onion
    OR: 2 tablespoons finely chopped onion
2 pimientos, chopped

1 Sauté rice in butter or margarine in frying pan with handle that will take oven heat, stirring often, just until golden; stir in bouillon, water, onion and pimientos; heat to boiling; cover.
2 Bake in moderate oven (375°) 40 minutes, or until rice is tender and liquid is absorbed.

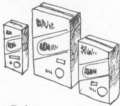

Saffron Rice Bake
Bake at 350° for 1 hour. Makes 6 servings

1 cup uncooked regular rice
3 tablespoons vegetable oil
1 large onion, chopped (1 cup)
1 clove garlic, minced
6 to 8 strands saffron
2½ cups hot water
3 envelopes instant vegetable broth
½ teaspoon salt
1 tablespoon Worcestershire sauce
    Few drops liquid red pepper seasoning
1 package (12 ounces) frozen deveined shelled raw shrimps

1 Sauté rice in vegetable oil, stirring constantly, until toasty-brown in a large frying pan; push to one side. Add onion and garlic and sauté until soft.
2 Combine saffron with hot water in a 4-cup measure; let stand a few minutes, then stir in vegetable broth, salt, Worcestershire sauce and red pepper seasoning. Stir into rice mixture with shrimps.
3 Heat to boiling; spoon into an 8-cup baking dish; cover.
4 Bake in moderate oven (350°) 1 hour, or until liquid is absorbed and rice is tender. Pull a few shrimps to the top for a garnish, if you wish.

Triple Green Rice
Flavor secrets: Green onions, chives, and zesty cheese.
Makes 4 servings

¼ cup chopped green onions
1 tablespoon cut chives
3 tablespoons butter or margarine
1⅓ cups precooked rice
½ teaspoon salt
1⅓ cups boiling water
½ cup grated Romano cheese
2 tablespoons chopped parsley

1 Sauté green onions and chives in butter or margarine until soft in a medium-size frying pan. Stir in rice, salt and boiling water; cover. Let stand 8 minutes, or until liquid is absorbed.
2 Sprinkle with cheese and parsley; toss to mix. Spoon into a serving bowl; garnish with parsley, if you wish.

Baked Curried Rice
Flavor is light and spicy—just right with veal, ham, or pork.
Bake at 350° for 45 minutes. Makes 6 servings

1 medium-size onion, chopped (½ cup)
¼ cup seedless raisins
¼ teaspoon curry powder
2 tablespoons butter or margarine
1 can (14 ounces) chicken broth
¼ cup water
½ teaspoon salt
    Dash of pepper
1 cup uncooked regular rice

1 Sauté onion with raisins and curry powder in butter or margarine until onion is soft in a medium-size frying pan. Stir in chicken broth, water, salt and pepper; heat to boiling; pour over rice in a 4-cup baking dish; cover.
2 Bake in moderate oven (350°) 45 minutes, or until rice is tender and liquid is absorbed; fluff with a fork.

1437

Javanese Fried Rice
Cooked rice sautés best if chilled overnight so grains are fluffy-dry.
Makes 6 servings

2 cups water
1 envelope instant vegetable broth
    OR: 1 vegetable-bouillon cube
¼ teaspoon ground cumin
1 cup uncooked regular rice
1 medium-size onion, chopped (½ cup)
½ clove of garlic, minced

3 tablespoons vegetable oil
½ teaspoon salt
¼ teaspoon chili powder
⅛ teaspoon ground mace

1 Heat water with vegetable broth or bouillon cube and cumin to boiling in a medium-size saucepan; stir in rice; cover. Cook 15 minutes, or just until rice is tender and liquid is absorbed. Spoon into a bowl; chill.
2 When ready to finish dish, sauté onion and garlic in 1 tablespoon of the vegetable oil until soft in a medium-size frying pan; remove and set aside.
3 Turn rice out onto paper toweling; fluff with a fork to separate grains. Sauté lightly in same frying pan, adding remaining 2 tablespoons vegetable oil.
4 Stir in onion mixture and seasonings; cover; heat slowly just until hot. Spoon into a heated serving bowl. Garnish with parsley and serve with toasted slivered almonds, chopped radishes and sliced green onions to sprinkle on top, if you wish.

Spanish Rice and Meat Balls
Makes 4 servings

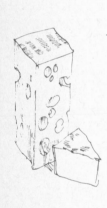

4 slices bacon
1 pound ground beef
1 egg
½ cup soft bread crumbs (1 slice)
2 teaspoons salt
1 large onion, chopped (1 cup)
½ cup chopped celery
½ cup chopped green pepper
1 teaspoon chili powder
1 cup uncooked regular rice
1 can (about 1 pound) tomatoes
1 cup water

1 Sauté bacon until crisp in a large frying pan; remove and drain on paper toweling.
2 Mix ground beef lightly with egg, bread crumbs and 1 teaspoon of the salt until well blended; shape into 16 small balls.
3 Brown in bacon drippings in same pan; push to one side.
4 Stir onion, celery, green pepper and chili powder into pan; sauté just until vegetables are soft.
5 Stir in rice, tomatoes, water and remaining salt; heat to boiling, stirring lightly to mix; cover.
6 Simmer, adding more water if mixture seems dry, 45 minutes, or until rice is tender and liquid is absorbed. Garnish with reserved bacon.

1438

Porcupines
Makes 6 servings

1 egg
½ cup water
1 envelope onion-soup mix
1½ pounds ground beef
½ cup uncooked regular rice
1 can (46 ounces) tomato juice
1 teaspoon sugar

1 Beat egg slightly with water and 2 tablespoons of the soup mix. Mix lightly with ground beef and ¼ cup of the rice; shape into 12 balls. Roll in remaining ¼ cup rice, pressing it lightly into meat.
2 Heat tomato juice to boiling; stir in remaining onion-soup mix and sugar. Place meat balls in sauce; cover.
3 Simmer, stirring several times, 50 minutes, or until rice puffs out around meat and is tender.

Risotto alla Milanese
This is a continental specialty that can be ready for the table in less than 1 hour.
Makes 6 servings

4 slices bacon, diced
1 pound chicken livers, halved
¼ cup sifted all-purpose flour
1 teaspoon salt
¼ teaspoon pepper
1 large onion, chopped (1 cup)
1 cup uncooked regular rice
2 envelopes or teaspoons instant chicken broth
1 teaspoon leaf basil, crumbled
1 bay leaf
2½ cups water
Chopped parsley

1 Cook bacon until crisp in a large skillet. Remove bacon with a slotted spoon and reserve.
2 Shake chicken livers in a plastic bag with flour, salt and pepper.
3 Brown chicken livers in bacon drippings. Remove with slotted spoon and reserve.
4 Sauté onion in same skillet until soft. (If there is no fat remaining in the skillet, add 2 tablespoons vegetable oil.) Stir in rice, chicken broth, basil, bay leaf and water.
5 Heat to boiling. Lower heat; stir rice mixture well; cover.
6 Simmer 10 minutes. Spoon browned chicken livers over rice. Return cover and simmer 20 minutes longer, or until liquid is absorbed and rice is tender; remove bay leaf. Sprinkle with reserved bacon and chopped parsley.

Olive Risotto

Simple molding trick gives this delicately seasoned rice fancy a trim shape.
Makes 8 servings

    1 large onion, chopped (1 cup)
    4 tablespoons (½ stick) butter or margarine
 1½ cups uncooked regular rice
    2 envelopes instant chicken broth
       OR: 2 chicken-bouillon cubes
    ½ teaspoon salt
    ½ teaspoon leaf rosemary, crumbled
 3½ cups water
    1 cup stuffed green olives, sliced

1 Sauté onion in butter or margarine until soft in a large saucepan. Stir in rice; cook, stirring constantly, 3 minutes, or until rice is well coated with butter mixture.
2 Stir in chicken broth or bouillon cubes, salt, rosemary and water. Heat to boiling, crushing bouillon cubes, if used, with a spoon; cover.
3 Cook slowly 30 minutes, or until rice is tender and liquid is absorbed; fold in sliced olives.
4 Spoon hot rice mixture into a 6-cup mold, packing down gently with back of spoon; let stand several minutes, then invert onto a heated serving plate.

TWO RICE DESSERTS

Eight Precious Pudding
Makes 8 servings

    1 cup uncooked regular rice
    ¼ cup sugar
    2 cups milk
    1 cup pitted dried prunes
    1 tablespoon chopped preserved ginger
    8 thin wedges candied pineapple
    8 mandarin-orange segments
    2 preserved kumquats, sliced
    2 pitted dates, quartered
    4 maraschino cherries, halved
    8 whole blanched almonds
       TART LEMON SAUCE (recipe follows)

1 Cook rice, following label directions; stir in sugar and milk. Heat to boiling, then simmer, stirring several times, 20 minutes, or until milk is absorbed completely; remove from heat.
2 Chop prunes; mix with ginger in a bowl.
3 Generously coat a 6-cup melon mold with butter or margarine. Arrange pineapple, mandarin-orange segments, kumquats, dates, cherries and almonds in a pretty pattern in bottom of mold.
4 Carefully spoon half of the rice mixture in an even layer over fruits; spread prune mixture over rice; spoon in remaining rice. Cover with foil or a double thickness of wax paper; fasten with string to hold tightly.
5 Place on a rack or trivet in a kettle or steamer; pour in boiling water to three fourths the depth of mold; cover tightly. Steam 1 hour. (Keep water boiling gently during entire cooking time, adding more boiling water, if needed.)
6 Cool pudding in mold 5 minutes; invert onto a large serving plate. Serve warm with TART LEMON SAUCE.

TART LEMON SAUCE—Mix ½ cup sugar, 2 tablespoons cornstarch and a dash of salt in a small saucepan; stir in ¾ cup water. Cook, stirring constantly, until mixture thickens and boils 3 minutes; remove from heat. Stir in 1 tablespoon butter or margarine until melted and ¼ cup lemon juice. Serve warm. Makes about 1⅓ cups.

Currant Rice Roll-Ups
Snowy sugar tops fluffy jelly-filled rice pancakes.
Makes 6 servings

    3 eggs, separated
    1 teaspoon sugar
    ½ teaspoon salt
    1 cup milk
    ½ cup sifted all-purpose flour
    1 tablespoon butter or margarine, melted
    1 cup cooked rice
    ¾ cup red currant jelly
      10X (confectioners' powdered) sugar

1 Beat egg yolks slightly with sugar, salt and milk in a medium-size bowl; beat in flour until smooth, then stir in melted butter or margarine; fold in cooked rice.
2 Beat egg whites until they form soft peaks in a medium-size bowl; fold into rice mixture.
3 Pour batter, ⅓ cup at a time, onto a heated lightly greased griddle or into a lightly greased large frying pan; spread into a 5-inch cake. Bake 3 minutes, or until top appears dry and underside is golden; turn; bake 2 minutes longer. Repeat to make 12 pancakes.
4 As each pancake is baked, spread with 1 tablespoon of the currant jelly; roll up, jelly-roll fashion; place on a serving platter. Keep warm until all are baked. Just before serving, sprinkle with 10X sugar and garnish with a twist of lemon, if you wish.

1439

PASTRY CHEF

PASTRY CHEF:
SOME RECIPES FOR CREAM PUFFS,
ECLAIRS AND OTHER PASTRIES,
HOW TO MAKE CREAM PUFF SWANS,
STEP-BY-STEP TO PERFECT
STRUDEL

Cream puffs . . . profiteroles . . . eclairs . . .
Napoleons . . . the whole range of wispy, crispy,
cream-filled, frosted French pastries can actually be made at home. So can a fine and flaky
strudel. And most of them more easily than you
suspect. It's true that the majority of these lavish
pastry recipes aren't for beginners. But any
woman with a modicum of experience and a
"feel for food" can make them without difficulty.

The recipes on the following pages make the
pastry line-up seem less formidable because
they show, in explicit step-by-step instructions,
how to mix, roll, shape and decorate pastries
with truly professional results. If you're nervous
about making fancy pastries, we suggest that
you begin with an easy recipe—cream puffs, for
example. After they have come from the oven,
poufed and browned, after they have been filled
with custard or cream filling and, perhaps, drizzled with frosting, you'll be inspired to try some
of the more intricate pastry recipes. And, need-
less to say, family and friends will thank you
for it.

Conversation piece: a lofty tower of Profiteroles.

SOME RECIPES USING
CREAM PUFF BATTER

Basic Cream Puff Batter
Recipe divides in half easily for making Profiteroles.

1 cup water
½ cup (1 stick) butter or margarine
1 cup sifted all-purpose flour
¼ teaspoon salt
4 eggs

1 Heat water and butter or margarine to boiling
in a medium-size heavy saucepan. Add flour and
salt all at once; stir vigorously with a wooden
spoon until batter forms a thick smooth ball that
follows spoon around pan; remove from heat
at once.
2 Beat in eggs, one at a time, beating well after
each addition, until batter is shiny-smooth.

Profiteroles
Such delectable dainties! Miniature puffs are
filled with ice cream, then crowned with dark
chocolate sauce.
Bake at 400° for 25 minutes. Makes 10 servings

1441

½ *recipe* BASIC CREAM PUFF BATTER *(recipe precedes)*
1 *quart vanilla ice cream*
FUDGY SAUCE *(recipe follows)*

1 Make BASIC CREAM PUFF BATTER.
2 Spoon in small mounds, a rounded teaspoonful for each, 2 inches apart, on ungreased cookie sheets. (Measure carefully so puffs will be about the same size.)
3 Bake in hot oven (400°) 25 minutes, or until puffed, crisp and golden. Remove carefully from cookie sheets; cool completely on wire racks.
4 When ready to fill, split puffs; spoon a tablespoon of vanilla ice cream into each; press tops back in place.
5 Pile into a shallow serving bowl; drizzle with warm FUDGY SAUCE. (To hold for serving later, place filled puffs in a single layer on cookie sheets, cover and store in freezer. Let stand at room temperature 10 to 15 minutes before serving to soften.)

FUDGY SAUCE—Combine 1 package (8 ounces) semisweet chocolate and ⅔ cup water in a small heavy saucepan; heat slowly, stirring often, until chocolate melts; stir in ½ cup sugar. Heat, stirring constantly, to boiling, then cook 5 minutes; stir in 4 tablespoons (½ stick) butter or margarine until melted. Serve warm. Makes about 1½ cups.

Beignets
Dainty French doughnuts turn dessert-fancy with a sparkly-golden fruit topper.
Makes 8 to 10 servings

1 *recipe* BASIC CREAM PUFF BATTER *(recipe precedes)*
Vegetable shortening or vegetable oil for frying
APRICOT-ALMOND SAUCE *(recipe follows)*

1 Make BASIC CREAM PUFF BATTER.
2 Melt enough vegetable shortening or pour in enough vegetable oil to make a 3-inch depth in an electric deep-fat fryer or large saucepan; heat to 400°.
3 Drop batter, a heaping teaspoonful at a time, into hot fat; fry, a few at a time and turning often, 5 minutes, or until puffed and golden. Lift out with a slotted spoon and drain on paper toweling; keep warm until all are cooked.
4 When ready to serve, place 3 or 4 on each serving plate; drizzle with warm APRICOT-ALMOND SAUCE.

APRICOT-ALMOND SAUCE—Combine 1 jar (12 ounces) apricot preserves with 2 tablespoons water in a small saucepan; heat slowly just to boiling. Press through a sieve, then return to saucepan; stir in 2 tablespoons light corn syrup and ¼ teaspoon almond extract. Makes 1 cup.

Strawberry-Cream Tower
Jumbo custardlike pancakes are layered with sweetened berries for this melt-in-your-mouth treat.
Makes 8 servings

1 *recipe* BASIC CREAM PUFF BATTER *(recipe precedes)*
¼ *cup sugar*
2 *teaspoons grated lemon peel*
1 *cup cream for whipping*
3 *tablespoons butter or margarine*
1 *pint strawberries, washed, hulled, sliced and sweetened*
1 *tablespoon 10X (confectioners' powdered) sugar*

1 Make BASIC CREAM PUFF BATTER; stir in sugar and lemon peel.
2 Beat cream until stiff in a medium-size bowl; fold into cream-puff mixture.
3 Melt 1 tablespoon of the butter or margarine in a 7-inch heavy frying pan, tilting pan to coat bottom and side. Spoon a third of the batter into pan, then spread into an even layer. Cook over low heat 8 minutes.
4 Turn this way: Tip pan and slide pancake onto a serving plate; invert pan over plate and turn rightside up. (Pancake will fall back into pan, unbaked side down.)
5 Bake 8 minutes longer, or until puffed and golden. Remove to a cookie sheet; keep warm.
6 Repeat with remaining batter, buttering pan between bakings, to make two more pancakes.
7 When ready to serve, stack pancakes with strawberries between on a heated serving platter; press 10X sugar through a sieve on top. Garnish with a whole strawberry, if you wish. Cut into wedges; serve warm.

Cream Puffs
Bake at 400° for 45 minutes. Makes 1 dozen

1 *recipe* BASIC CREAM PUFF BATTER *(recipe precedes)*
2 *recipes* CUSTARD CREAM *(recipe follows) or any favorite custard pudding, sweetened whipped cream or ice cream*
10X (confectioners' powdered) sugar

1 Make BASIC CREAM PUFF BATTER. Spoon into 12 mounds, using 1 heaping serving table-

Two cream puff-batter-based beauties: Beignets (bottom) and upstaging them, Strawberry-Cream Tower.

spoonful for each, 2 inches apart on ungreased cookie sheets.

2 Bake in hot oven (400°) 45 minutes or until puffed, crisp and lightly golden. Remove from cookie sheets with a spatula; cool completely on wire racks.

3 Just before serving, cut a slice across top of each cream puff and lift off. Scoop out any bits of soft dough from bottoms with tip of teaspoon. Fill with CUSTARD CREAM or your choice of custard pudding, sweetened whipped cream or ice cream. Sprinkle tops with 10X sugar.

HOW TO MAKE CREAM PUFF SWANS

What perky dessert show-offs! Fill with ice cream and serve with a sparkling sauce, as pictured, or use a creamy pudding or flavored whipped-cream filling. BASIC CREAM PUFF BATTER *(recipe precedes)* will make eight swans—just right for a party.

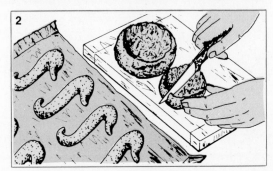

Start with a pattern for swan heads
Draw a simple pattern about 4 inches long on cardboard, cut it out, then trace onto a foil-covered cookie sheet. A wax pencil or crayon will brighten the outline, but a plain pencil will work, too. (Picture below shows pattern head down.) Allow at least 3 inches between each head. Now mix up BASIC CREAM PUFF BATTER, and you're ready.

1 Attach plain tip to a pastry bag; fill bag with batter. Starting at beak, squeeze out batter, making double circle for head. Bake heads at 400° for 20 minutes. Bake rest of batter in 8 even-size mounds on second ungreased cookie sheet for about 45 minutes; cool.

1444

2 Cut a thin caplike circle from top of each round puff, then halve it to make the two wings. Scoop out any soft bits of dough from bottom with a teaspoon so shell will hold as much filling as possible. Dainty heads need no attention, so swans are now ready to assemble.

3 Spoon just enough ice cream into shell to make an anchor for head. Set head in place, as shown; add more ice cream to fill shell generously. Stick wings into ice cream at a jaunty angle and your swan is ready to sail away to your table. Add sauce as you wish.

Raspberry Ribbon Bread

This coffeetime specialty boasts a layer of flaky pastry topped with jam and curlicues of cream puff batter.

Bake at 400° for 45 minutes. Makes 16 servings

  2 cups sifted all-purpose flour
  1 teaspoon salt
  ⅔ cup vegetable shortening
  6 tablespoons cold water
  ½ cup raspberry jam (from a 12-ounce jar)
  1 recipe BASIC CREAM PUFF BATTER (recipe precedes)
    RUM GLAZE (recipe follows)

1 Sift flour and salt into a medium-size bowl; cut in shortening with a pastry blender until mixture is crumbly. Sprinkle water over, 1 tablespoon at a time; mix lightly with a fork just until pastry holds together and leaves side of bowl clean.
2 Roll out to a rectangle, 16x8, on a lightly floured pastry cloth or board; trim edges even. Cut in half lengthwise to make two 4-inch-wide strips; place, 2 inches apart, on an ungreased large cookie sheet. Spoon raspberry jam in a ribbon down middle of each; chill.
3 Make BASIC CREAM PUFF BATTER. Spoon into a pastry bag; attach a plain or fancy tip. Press batter out onto jam-topped pastry rectangles, zigzagging from side to side.
4 Bake in hot oven (400°) 45 minutes, or until puffed and golden. Remove carefully and place on wire racks; cool.
5 Drizzle with RUM GLAZE. Cut into 2-inch-wide pieces. Serve warm.

  RUM GLAZE—Blend ¾ cup 10X (confectioners' powdered) sugar, 1 tablespoon water and ½ teaspoon rum flavoring or extract until smooth in a small bowl. Makes about ⅓ cup.

Strawberry Cream Puff Cake

To cut down on the last-minute fuss, make the pastry base a day ahead.

Bake at 400° for 40 minutes. Makes 8 servings

Pastry and Cream Puff Base
  ½ package piecrust mix
  1 cup water
  ½ cup (1 stick) butter or margarine
  1 cup sifted all-purpose flour
  ½ teaspoon salt
  4 eggs

Filling
  3 eggs, separated
  2 cups milk
  1 package (about 3 ounces) vanilla pudding and pie filling mix
  3 teaspoons vanilla

  2 cups (1 pint) strawberries
  ½ cup sugar
  1 cup cream for whipping
    SUGAR GLAZE (recipe follows)

1 Make pastry base: Prepare piecrust mix, following label directions. Roll out to an 8-inch round on a lightly floured pastry cloth or board; trim edge even, using an 8-inch layer-cake pan as a guide. Place round on a large ungreased cookie sheet.
2 Heat water and butter or margarine to boiling in a medium-size saucepan. Add flour and salt all at once; stir vigorously with a wooden spoon 2 minutes, or until batter forms a thick smooth ball that follows spoon around pan. Remove from heat; cool slightly.
3 Beat in eggs, one at a time, until batter is shiny-smooth.
4 Attach a fluted tip to a pastry bag; spoon batter into bag. Press out part around edge of pastry to make a ring. (During baking, batter will puff up to form a rim around pastry.)
5 Draw an 8-inch round on a second ungreased cookie sheet; press out batter around edge to make a second ring. Press out remaining batter in 8 small mounds on same cookie sheet.
6 Bake all pastry in hot oven (400°) 40 minutes, or until puffed, crisp and golden. Cool completely on cookie sheets on wire racks.
7 Make filling: Beat egg yolks with milk in a small saucepan; stir in pudding mix. Cook, following label directions; remove from heat. Stir in 2 teaspoons of the vanilla; chill.
8 Wash strawberries; set aside 8 of the prettiest to glaze in Step 11. Hull remaining berries and slice into a medium-size bowl; stir in 2 tablespoons of the sugar. Beat cream with another 2 tablespoons sugar and remaining 1 teaspoon vanilla until stiff in a medium-size bowl.
9 Beat egg whites until foamy in a medium-size bowl; slowly beat in remaining ¼ cup sugar until meringue forms soft peaks; fold in chilled pudding mixture.
10 Assemble dessert: Place pastry base on a flat serving plate. Carefully cut a thin slice from top and set aside for nibbles. Arrange a row of strawberries around ring, then spread with cream (or press through a pastry bag) and cover with another row of strawberries; top with plain cream puff ring. Spoon pudding mixture into hollow in center; chill dessert and remaining whipped cream.
11 Make SUGAR GLAZE. Holding one whole strawberry at a time by its leafy tip, dip into hot syrup, turning to coat berry completely; place on a foil-covered wire rack. Let stand until cool and syrup is hardened.
12 Cut a thin slice from top of each small puff; dip bottoms, one at a time, into syrup; press

1445

around top of dessert. (Syrup will harden and hold them in place.) Spoon remaining whipped cream into puffs and in center of dessert. Garnish puffs with glazed strawberries. Chill no longer than 2 hours. Cut in wedges.

SUGAR GLAZE—Combine 2 cups sugar and 1 cup water in a small heavy saucepan. Heat slowly, stirring constantly, until sugar dissolves, then cook rapidly, without stirring, to 260° on a candy thermometer. (A teaspoonful of syrup will form a hard ball when dropped in cold water.) Remove from heat at once.

Spun-Gold Cream Pouf

Grandly French! A pastry ring and cream puffs are filled with custard and pistachio cream, then topped with a golden spun-sugar crown.
Bake at 400° for 40 minutes for ring, and 25 minutes for puffs. Makes 12 servings

Pastry
1 cup sifted all-purpose flour
3 tablespoons sugar
Dash of salt
6 tablespoons (¾ stick) butter or margarine
1 egg, slightly beaten

Cream Puffs
1 recipe BASIC CREAM PUFF BATTER (recipe precedes)

Custard Cream
¼ cup sugar
¼ cup cornstarch
1 teaspoon unflavored gelatin (from 1 envelope)
¼ teaspoon salt
3 eggs, separated
1½ cups milk
2 teaspoons vanilla

Pistachio Cream
1 cup cream for whipping
2 teaspoons sugar
½ teaspoon almond extract
2 tablespoons chopped pistachio nuts

Spun Sugar
¾ cup sugar
2 tablespoons light corn syrup
2 tablespoons water

1 Make pastry: Combine flour, sugar and salt in a medium-size bowl; cut in butter or margarine with a pastry blender until mixture is crumbly. Blend in egg with a fork, then knead a few times until smooth.
2 Roll out to a 10-inch round on a lightly floured pastry cloth or board; place on an ungreased cookie sheet; trim edge, using a dinner plate as a guide, to make a perfect round. Prick well all over with a fork; chill 30 minutes.

3 Make cream puffs. Attach a plain round tip to a pastry bag; fill bag with part of the batter; press out all around edge of pastry circle, as pictured. (It will take about ⅔ of batter for ring. When baked, batter will puff up to form a high rim around pastry.)
4 Shape remaining batter into 12 small puffs, using a level tablespoonful for each, and about 15 very small puffs, using a level teaspoonful for each, on two more ungreased cookie sheets.
5 Bake ring and puffs in hot oven (400°) 40 minutes for ring, and 25 minutes for puffs, or until all are puffed, crisp, and lightly golden. Cool pastry ring completely on cookie sheet set on a wire rack. Remove puffs with a spatula; cool completely on wire racks. (This much can be done a day ahead, if you wish.)
6 About 3 hours before serving, make custard cream: Mix sugar, cornstarch, gelatin and salt in the top of a small double boiler; stir in egg yolks and milk.
7 Cook, stirring constantly, over simmering water 10 minutes, or until gelatin dissolves and mixture coats a metal spoon; continue cooking, stirring once or twice, 5 minutes longer. Strain into a large bowl; stir in vanilla.
8 While custard mixture cooks, beat egg whites until they stand in firm peaks in a medium-size bowl; fold into hot custard mixture; chill.
9 Make pistachio cream: Beat cream with sugar and almond extract until stiff in a medium-size bowl; fold in pistachio nuts.
10 Split puffed ring on top of pastry and the 12 small puffs; fill all with pistachio cream; replace tops. (No need to fill the 15 very small puffs.)
11 Place ring on a flat serving plate; spoon chilled custard in center. Place small puffs

What you might call "the shortcake to end all short-cakes." It's super-showy Strawberry Cream Puff Cake.

around top edge and very small ones on custard in center. Chill.

12 About an hour before serving, make spun sugar: Mix sugar, corn syrup and water in a small heavy saucepan. Heat, stirring constantly, just until sugar dissolves, then cook rapidly, without stirring, to 360° on a candy thermometer and syrup is a light golden color; remove from heat at once. Let cool to 200°, or until syrup is thick and forms a long thread when dropped from a teaspoon.

13 Dip spoon into syrup; let a drop fall onto a cream puff, then lift spoon quickly, pulling the thread with your fingers into a long slender strand and looping it from puff to puff, building up into a heavy weblike cone. Repeat with more syrup, topping each cream puff around edge before pulling and looping thread.

14 Cut into wedges. Let dessert stand at room temperature until serving time.

Scandinavian Ribbon Torte

Just luscious! Ten spicy thin cookie layers are stacked with chocolate-cream and jam fillings, then frosted with chocolate.

Bake at 350° for 12 minutes. Makes 12 servings

> 1 cup (2 sticks) butter or margarine (for cookie layers)
> 1 cup sugar
> 2 eggs
> 1¾ cups sifted all-purpose flour
> 2 teaspoons ground cinnamon
> 1 cup cream for whipping
> 9 squares sweet cooking chocolate (from a 4-ounce package)
> ½ cup raspberry jam, sieved
> 1 teaspoon butter or margarine (for topping)

1 Cream butter or margarine with sugar until fluffy in a medium-size bowl; beat in eggs, one at a time, then stir in flour and cinnamon.

2 Cut ten 8-inch rounds of wax paper, using a layer-cake pan as a guide; place, two at a time, on a large cookie sheet; brush with melted butter or margarine. (If you have two cookie sheets, use both, so you can bake 4 rounds at a time.) Spread about ⅓ cup batter on each round just to edge to make a thin layer. (Tip: You might find the job easier—and faster—if you place the paper round on the back of the layer-cake pan, butter, spread with batter, then slide off onto the cookie sheet.)

3 Bake in moderate oven (350°) 12 minutes, or until golden. Let cool a few minutes on cookie sheet until firm, then remove carefully; peel off paper; cool layers completely on wire racks.

(Layers can be made a day ahead, if you wish, and stacked with wax paper or foil between until ready to fill. Handle them carefully, as they are very crisp.)

4 Cool cookie sheets, then repeat with remaining batter and wax-paper rounds to make 10 layers in all.

5 About 2 hours before serving, beat cream until stiff in a medium-size bowl; grate 2 squares of the chocolate and fold in. (Set remaining chocolate and about ½ cup of the cream mixture aside for topping.)

6 Place 1 cookie layer on a flat serving plate; spread with about ⅓ cup of the chocolate cream; top with a second cookie layer; spread with 2 tablespoons of the sieved raspberry jam. Repeat with remaining cookie layers, alternating chocolate-cream and jam fillings; leave top plain.

7 Melt remaining 7 squares chocolate with the 1 teaspoon butter or margarine in a cup over hot water; spread on top of cake; chill. Just before serving, garnish with saved chocolate cream, and red raspberries, if you wish.

Note—To make the fresh-looking raspberry garnish, thaw a package of frozen raspberries just enough so you can pick out the choicest whole ones. Stand them, not touching, in a shallow pan; refreeze until serving time.

ECLAIRS AND OTHER PASTRIES

Eclairs

Your pastry bag presses out the eclair forms; the filling starts with made-from-scratch candy brittle.

Bake at 400° for 25 minutes. Makes 3 dozen

> 1 recipe BASIC CREAM PUFF BATTER (recipe precedes)
> ALMOND FILLING (recipe follows)
> 2 cups sifted 10X (confectioners' powered) sugar
> 3 tablespoons freshly brewed strong coffee
> 3 squares unsweetened chocolate

1 Make BASIC CREAM PUFF BATTER. Attach a plain round tip to a pastry bag; fill bag with batter. Press out into thin strips, 3 inches long and 1 inch apart, onto ungreased cookie sheets.

2 Bake in hot oven (400°) 25 minutes, or until puffed and lightly golden. Remove carefully from cookie sheets to wire racks; cool completely.

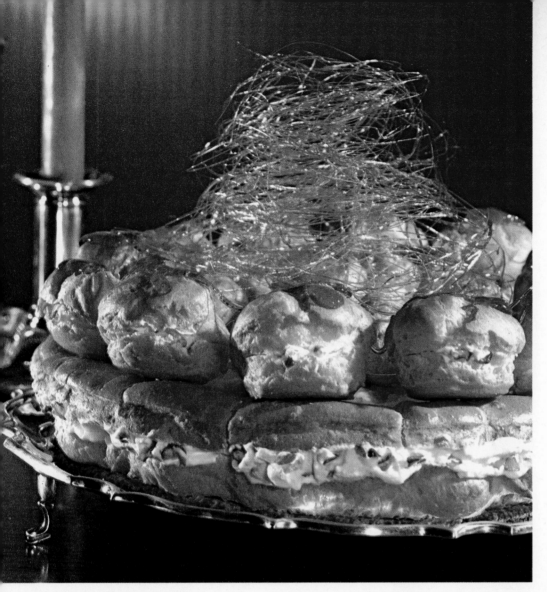

One of the world's great glamour desserts—Spun-Gold Cream Pouf, filled with two creams and topped with a swirling spun-sugar cloud.

1449

A crispy, spicy, ten (count them) layer cookie stack, put together with chocolate cream and tart jam. It's Scandinavian Ribbon Torte.

3 Cut a thin slice lengthwise from top of each eclair; lift off. Spoon 1 rounded tablespoonful ALMOND FILLING into each eclair; replace tops.
4 Beat 10X sugar with coffee until smooth in a small bowl; spread over eclairs to glaze lightly; let stand until glaze is firm.
5 Melt chocolate in a cup over hot water; drizzle in ribbons over coffee glaze. Chill until serving time.

Almond Filling

The almond candy that flavors the filling can be made ahead, if you like.
Makes enough to fill 3 dozen tiny eclairs

  ½ cup sliced blanched almonds
  ½ cup sugar (for almond candy)
  2 tablespoons water
  ⅔ cup sugar (for filling)
  4 tablespoons cornstarch
  3 tablespoons all-purpose flour
  ½ teaspoon salt
2½ cups milk
  2 egg yolks
  2 tablespoons butter or margarine
1½ teaspoons vanilla

1 Spread almonds in a shallow baking pan. Toast in moderate oven (350°), shaking pan several times, 12 minutes, or until lightly browned.
2 Combine the ½ cup sugar and water in a medium-size saucepan; heat slowly, stirring constantly, until sugar melts and mixture turns golden. Quickly stir in almonds until coated.
3 Spread at once on a buttered cookie sheet; let stand until firm. Break mixture into small pieces; place in a transparent bag; crush to powder with a rolling pin. Set aside for Step 6.
4 Combine the ⅔ cup sugar, cornstarch, flour and salt in a large saucepan; stir in milk. Cook slowly, stirring constantly, until mixture thickens and boils 3 minutes.
5 Beat egg yolks slightly in a small bowl; slowly stir in ½ cup of the hot mixture; stir back into remaining mixture in saucepan. Cook, stirring constantly, 3 minutes; remove from heat.
6 Stir in butter or margarine and vanilla; cool. Stir in almond powder; chill.

1450

Strawberry Cornucopias

Cookies must be warm to shape into cones, so bake them only two at a time. Recipe tells how to make shaping forms.
Bake at 375° for 5 minutes. Makes 30

  2 egg whites
  ⅓ cup sugar
  ½ cup sifted all-purpose flour
  4 tablespoons (¼ stick) butter or margarine, melted and cooled
  ¼ cup ground blanched almonds
  1 teaspoon almond extract
  ½ cup red currant jelly
  2 pints strawberries, washed and hulled
  2 cups cream for whipping
    Red food coloring

1 Make forms for shaping cookies this way: Cut two 4-inch circles from thin cardboard; curl into cornucopia shapes; fasten with transparent tape. Cover outsides with foil.
2 Beat egg whites until foamy-white and double in volume in a small bowl; beat in sugar, 1 tablespoon at a time, beating all the time, until meringue stands in firm peaks.
3 Stir in flour, alternately with melted butter or margarine, until smooth; fold in almonds and almond extract.
4 Drop batter, 2 teaspoonsful for each cookie, 4 inches apart, on a greased small cookie sheet; spread into a thin 3-inch round. (Make only 2 cookies at a time as they must be shaped while hot. To speed the job, use two cookie sheets and bake one batch while shaping the other.)
5 Bake in moderate oven (375°) 5 minutes, or until delicately browned around edges but still white in center.
6 Loosen cookies carefully with a spatula; shape around foil-covered cones to make cornucopias; remove carefully from form and cool completely on a wire rack. (Work quickly as cookies harden fast. If they become too brittle to shape easily, return cookie sheet to oven for about 30 seconds to soften them.)
7 Heat currant jelly until melted in a small saucepan; cool. Holding each strawberry on a fork, dip into melted jelly to coat completely; stand, flat end down, on a plate. Chill until jelly is firm.
8 Beat cream with a few drops red food coloring until stiff in a medium-size bowl; spoon onto cookie cones to fill. (Or press through a pastry bag.) Press a glazed strawberry into top of each cone; chill; (Fill cones no longer than 2 hours before serving as cream tends to soften them.)

Lemon Tartlets Véronique

Cookielike shells hold mellow lemon filling, glazed grapes. Pretty fruits for another time: strawberries, peach slices.
Bake shells at 375° for 22 minutes. Makes 1 dozen

Fancy pastries and oh-so-French. (L. to r.): Parisian Party Cakes, Madeleines a la Marcel, Strawberry Cornucopias, Lemon Tartlets Veronique, Pistachio Pinwheels and Eclairs with squiggles of melted chocolate. Yes, you can make them.

2 cups sifted all-purpose flour
3 tablespoons sugar
½ teaspoon salt
½ cup (1 stick) butter or margarine
¼ cup vegetable shortening
6 tablespoons water
  LEMON FILLING (recipe follows)
1 pound seedless green grapes, stemmed and halved
1 cup apple jelly, melted and cooled
1 cup cream for whipping

1 Sift flour, sugar and salt into a medium-size bowl. Cut in butter or margarine and shortening with a pastry blender until mixture is crumbly.
2 Sprinkle water over top; mix lightly with a fork until pastry holds together and leaves side of bowl clean. Turn out onto a lightly floured pastry cloth or board; knead just until smooth; divide into 12 even pieces. Chill dough at least an hour for easier handling.
3 Press each piece of dough into a fluted 3-inch tart-shell pan to cover bottom and side evenly.

Fit a small piece of wax paper over pastry in each pan; pour uncooked rice or beans on top to hold pastry in place during baking. Set pans in a large shallow pan for easy handling.

4 Bake in moderate oven (375°) 10 minutes; remove from oven. Lift out wax paper and rice or beans; return pans to oven. Bake 12 minutes longer, or until pastry is golden. Cool shells completely in pans on wire racks, then remove carefully from pans.

5 Spoon LEMON FILLING into each shell; arrange grape halves, cut sides up, on top to form rosettes; brush grapes with apple jelly; chill.

6 Just before serving, beat cream until stiff in a medium-size bowl. Attach a fancy tip to a pastry bag; fill bag with whipped cream; press out in tiny rosettes on top of tartlets. Chill until serving time.

LEMON FILLING—Beat 6 eggs slightly in the top of a large double boiler; stir in 1 cup sugar, ½ cup (1 stick) butter or margarine, 2 teaspoons grated lemon peel and ⅓ cup lemon juice. Cook, stirring constantly, over hot, *not boiling*, water 15 minutes, or until very thick. Pour into a medium-size bowl; cover; chill. Makes 3 cups.

Parisian Party Cakes

Little cakes, each barely two bites—but with apricot glaze, creamy frosting, and almonds, they're definitely rich ones.
Bake at 350° for 20 minutes. Makes 2 dozen tiny cakes

4 tablespoons (½ stick) butter or margarine
6 eggs
1 cup sugar
1 teaspoon vanilla
1 cup sifted cake flour
1 can (3½ ounces) sliced almonds
1 jar (12 ounces) apricot preserves
4 tablespoons light rum
MOCHA BUTTER CREAM (recipe follows)
FROSTING ROSES and LEAVES
(recipe follows)

1 Grease a baking pan, 15x10x1; flour lightly, tapping out any excess.

2 Melt butter or margarine over low heat in a small saucepan; remove from heat. Pour into a cup; let stand until solids settle to bottom.

3 Beat eggs with sugar in the top of a double boiler; place over simmering water. (Do not let water boil or touch bottom of pan.) Heat, stirring constantly, 10 minutes, or until sugar dissolves and mixture warms slightly; pour into a large bowl.

4 Beat with an electric beater at high speed 10 minutes, or until mixture is very thick and triple in volume; beat in vanilla.

5 Measure 3 tablespoonsful of the clear liquid butter or margarine into a cup; discard solids.

6 Fold flour into egg mixture, a third at a time, alternately with the liquid butter or margarine, just until blended. Pour into prepared pan, spreading evenly.

7 Bake in moderate oven (350°) 20 minutes, or until center springs back when lightly pressed with fingertip. Cool 10 minutes in pan on a large wire rack. Loosen around edges with a spatula; turn out onto rack, working spatula gently under bottom of cake, if needed, to loosen. Cool cake completely. Cut lengthwise into sixths, then crosswise into eighths to make 48 pieces.

8 While cake bakes, spread almonds in a shallow pan; toast in same oven 12 minutes, or until lightly golden; cool. Place in a plastic bag; crush lightly with a rolling pin; spread in a pie plate.

9 Press apricot preserves through a sieve into a small saucepan; heat slowly to boiling; stir in rum. Brush over tops and sides of each piece of cake.

10. Frost tops of half of the pieces with MOCHA BUTTER CREAM; top each, sandwich style, with an unfrosted piece, apricot side up. Frost sides of cakes; dip in toasted almonds; place in a single layer on a cookie sheet. Frost tops of cakes.

11 Trim each cake with a FROSTING ROSE and several LEAVES. Chill cakes until serving time.

Mocha Butter Cream

Frosting classic the French reserve for fine cakes and elegant occasions.
Makes enough to frost 2 dozen tiny cakes

1 cup (2 sticks) butter or margarine
5 squares semisweet chocolate
¼ cup freshly brewed strong coffee
⅔ cup sugar
⅛ teaspoon cream of tartar
⅓ cup water
5 egg yolks

1 Soften butter or margarine to room temperature; cut each stick into 8 pieces.

2 Combine chocolate and coffee in the top of a small double boiler; heat over hot water, stirring several times, until chocolate melts and mixture is smooth; cool to lukewarm.

3 Combine sugar, cream of tartar and water in a small heavy saucepan; heat, stirring con-

1452

stantly, to boiling, then cook rapidly, without stirring, to 238° on a candy thermometer. (A teaspoonful of syrup will form a soft ball when dropped in cold water.) Cool to lukewarm.

4 Beat egg yolks until fluffy in a large bowl with electric mixer at high speed; slowly beat in sugar syrup until completely blended.

5 Beat in butter or margarine, 1 piece at a time, until frosting is thick and fluffy; beat in the cooled chocolate mixture.

Note—If frosting is not used immediately, cover and chill. Remove from refrigerator about 10 minutes before spreading on cakes and let stand at room temperature to soften, then beat until fluffy again.

Frosting Roses and Leaves

If you find you have some frosting left, cover with a damp paper towel and chill to use on your next baking day.

Makes enough to trim 2 dozen tiny cakes

½ *cup (1 stick) butter or margarine*
1 *package (1 pound) 10X (confectioners' pow-dered) sugar, sifted*
1 *egg white*
1 *tablespoon light cream or table cream*
    Dash of salt
1 *teaspoon vanilla*
    Green and red food colorings

1 Cream butter or margarine until soft in large bowl of electric mixer. Beat in 10X sugar, alternately with unbeaten egg white and cream, with mixer at low speed; beat in salt and vanilla.

2 Increase speed to medium and continue beating until frosting is fluffy-smooth.

3 Spoon one quarter of the frosting into a small bowl; tint green with a few drops food coloring; cover with a damp paper towel until ready to use. Tint remaining frosting pink with red food coloring.

4 To make roses: Cut 24 small squares of wax paper; place one on the bottom end of a small glass, holding in place with a dot of frosting. (This makes a handy turntable to speed the job.)

5 Fit a flower tip onto a cake-decorating set; fill with pink frosting. Hold decorator horizontally with wide end of tip at center of wax paper, and gently and evenly press out frosting, turning glass at the same time, to make a tight center for rose. Continue pressing frosting around center in short overlapping strokes to make enough petals to form a full-blown rose. Re-

move paper from glass; place on a cookie sheet. Repeat to make 24 roses in all; chill. To remove from paper, loosen gently with a spatula; lift off.

6 To make leaves: Fit leaf tip onto cake-decorating set; fill with green frosting from Step 3. Press out in tiny leaf shapes directly onto cakes.

Ribbon Jewel Cakes

Unusual little pastries of five thin layers, baked on the back of a pan, filled and frosted with an array of flavors.

Bake at 350° for 10 minutes. Makes 32 tiny cakes

4 *eggs*
1 *cup (2 sticks) butter or margarine*
1 *cup sugar*
2 *cups sifted all-purpose flour*
1 *can (5 ounces) toasted slivered almonds*
1 *cup (8-ounce carton) dairy sour cream*
½ *cup apricot preserves*
½ *cup red raspberry preserves*
    BUTTER CREAM FROSTING *(recipe follows)*
1 *square semisweet chocolate*
1½ *teaspoons vegetable shortening*

1 Butter the back of a baking pan, 13x9x2; dust lightly with flour, tapping off any excess.

2 Separate eggs, placing whites in a medium-size bowl and yolks in a custard cup. Beat egg whites until they form soft peaks.

3 Cream butter or margarine with sugar until fluffy-light in a large bowl; beat in egg yolks. Stir in flour just until blended; stir in beaten egg whites.

4 Measure about ⅔ cup of the batter; spread on prepared pan almost to edge to make a thin layer.

5 Bake in moderate oven (350°) 10 minutes, or just until golden-brown around edges; carefully remove entire layer and cool on a large wire rack. Cool pan; wash, butter and flour back between each of four more bakings.

6 Grind or chop almonds very fine; stir into sour cream in a small bowl.

7 Place 1 cake layer, top side up, on a cutting board or cookie sheet; spread with ¼ cup apricot preserves, then with ⅓ cup sour-cream mixture. Add second cake layer and spread with ¼ cup raspberry preserves and ⅓ cup sour-cream mixture. Repeat, alternating apricot cream and raspberry cream between remaining layers, leaving top plain. Place a second board or flat pan on top to weigh down layers; chill overnight.

1453

8 Trim crust from edges; spread top with BUTTER CREAM FROSTING. Cut cake crosswise into 8 strips about 1½ inches wide; cut each strip crosswise into fourths to make 32 little cakes.
9 Melt semisweet chocolate and shortening in a cup over hot water; drizzle from a wooden pick in parallel lines over cakes. Using a clean pick, draw across lines to pull chocolate to make tiny squares. Chill cakes.

BUTTER CREAM FROSTING—Cream 3 tablespoons butter or margarine until soft in a medium-size bowl; stir in ¾ cup sifted 10X (confectioners' powdered) sugar, 1 tablespoon cream, dash of salt and 1 teaspoon vanilla. Slowly beat in about ¾ cup more 10X sugar until frosting is easy to spread. Makes about ¾ cup.

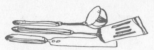

Pistachio Pinwheels
To make these tiny sweets, bake a thin jelly roll, cut it into strips, spread ruby-red jelly inside and out.
Bake at 400° for 6 minutes. Makes 8 small cakes

⅓ cup sifted cake flour
½ teaspoon baking powder
⅛ teaspoon salt
2 eggs
¼ cup sugar
¼ teaspoon vanilla
¼ teaspoon almond extract
½ cup red raspberry or strawberry jelly
3 tablespoons finely chopped pistachio nuts

1 Grease a baking pan, 15x10x1; line bottom with wax paper; grease paper lightly.
2 Measure flour, baking powder and salt into a sifter.
3 Beat eggs until foamy in a large bowl; slowly beat in sugar until thick and creamy; stir in vanilla and almond extract.
4 Sift flour mixture over top, then fold in; spread batter evenly in pan.
5 Bake in hot oven (400°) 6 minutes, or until center springs back when lightly pressed with fingertip. (Do not overbake or cake will be too crisp to roll.)
6 Loosen cake around edges with a knife; invert onto a towel sprinkled generously with more granulated sugar; peel off wax paper. Trim any crisp edges from cake. Starting at one end, roll up, jelly-roll fashion; cool completely on a wire rack.
7 When ready to finish desserts, unroll cake. Cut lengthwise into quarters; then halve each quarter crosswise to make 8 pieces.
8 Beat jelly with a fork in a small bowl. Spread a rounded teaspoonful over each piece of cake;

reroll tightly. Spread remaining jelly thinly over one end of each roll to cover about halfway; roll in pistachio nuts.

Madeleines à la Marcel
For French novelist Marcel Proust, madeleines were a sort of time machine, each feathery sweet bite catapulting him back to his childhood, when he first came to know madeleines. To make them, you'll need special little molds. Many department stores stock them, as do specialty and housewares shops.
Bake at 350° for 20 minutes. Makes 2 dozen

1 cup (2 sticks) butter or margarine
3 eggs
1 cup granulated sugar
1 teaspoon grated lemon peel
1 teaspoon vanilla
1½ cups sifted cake flour
½ cup red currant jelly
10X (confectioners' powdered) sugar

1 Butter madeleine molds well; dust with flour, tapping out any excess.
2 Melt the 1 cup butter or margarine over low heat in a small saucepan; remove from heat. Pour into a 1-cup measure; let stand until solids settle to bottom.
3 Beat eggs with granulated sugar and lemon peel in the top of a large double boiler; place over simmering water. (Do not let water boil or touch bottom of pan.) Beat mixture with an electric mixer at high speed 5 minutes until thick and light; remove from water. Pour into a large bowl; stir in vanilla.
4 Measure ¾ cup of the clear liquid butter or margarine into another cup; discard solids.
5 Fold flour into egg mixture, then fold in the liquid butter or margarine. Spoon into prepared molds, filling each half full. Place molds in a jelly-roll pan for easy handling. (Cover remaining batter and let stand at room temperature while baking first batch.)
6 Bake in moderate oven (350°) 20 minutes, or until tops spring back when lightly pressed with fingertip. Cool 5 minutes in molds on wire racks. Loosen around edges with the tip of a small knife; turn out onto racks, tapping gently, if needed, to loosen from bottom. Cool completely. Repeat Steps 5 and 6, washing and buttering molds between bakings, to make 48 madeleines in all. Store in a covered container until ready to fill.
7 About an hour before serving, beat currant jelly with a fork in a small bowl. Spread on the flat side of half of the madeleines; top each with a plain madeleine, flat side down. Dust lightly with 10X sugar.

Basic French Pastry

1 pound (4 sticks) butter or margarine, well chilled
4¼ cups sifted all-purpose flour
1 cup ice water
2 tablespoons lemon juice

1 Cut ½ pound (2 sticks) butter or margarine into flour in large bowl until mixture is crumbly and pale yellow. Use a pastry blender for easy chopping. (Keep remaining 2 sticks butter or margarine chilled for Step 4.)

2 Stir ice water and lemon juice all at once into crumbly mixture. Continue stirring with a fork until mixture is completely moistened and pastry is very stiff. Wrap in wax paper, foil or transparent wrap; chill 30 minutes.

3 Unwrap pastry and roll out to a rectangle, 18x12, on well-floured pastry cloth. Pastry

should be ¼ inch thick. (A cloth is better than a board, since the pastry is rich and slightly sticky as it is worked. A pastry cloth holds in the flour, so it mixes evenly into the pastry as it is rolled.) Roll straight, lifting the rolling pin each time as you reach the edge, so pastry will be evenly thick.

4 Slice saved ½ pound (2 sticks) very cold butter or margarine into thin even pats over two thirds of pastry to form a square about 12x12.

5 Fold uncovered third of pastry over middle third; fold opposite end over top. Then fold pastry in thirds crosswise to make a block. Now you have 9 layers of pastry with pats of butter or margarine between each. Roll out again to an even rectangle, 18x12; repeat folding as above; chill 30 minutes.

1455

6 Repeat rolling, folding, and chilling 3 more times. Pastry is stiff and cold, so first pound firmly with your rolling pin to flatten, watching carefully to keep thickness even. After rolling and folding the last time, wrap and chill pastry overnight, or several days, then shape, using the recipes that follow as your guide.

**Follow These Simple Rules
for Puff-Perfect French Pastry:**

1 Take butter or margarine from the refrigerator just before using. It must be well chilled.
2 Use ice water. Measure just before you add it.
3 Roll pastry just to edges—not over—to keep it evenly thick so it will puff evenly in baking.
4 Use a ruler to measure rectangles; cut lines straight. Use your sharpest long-blade knife for cutting.
5 Chill pastry well before each rolling, then chill again 30 minutes after shaping and before baking—one secret to its puffy, flaky, shattery crispness.
6 Cut off just the amount of pastry you'll need for each shaping. Keep the rest chilled. Avoid rerolling, as pastry will not puff as high or as

evenly. Don't waste the cuttings. Instead, shape with your hands into twists or rounds for canapé bases, or crispy treats with ice cream, cut-up fruit, pudding or coffee.
7 Follow baking directions carefully. High temperature at first, then lower temperature, are secrets to making pastry puff several times its height and bake crisply all the way through. Pastries should be a rich brown (the color of brown paper) when they come from the oven.
8 Bake pastries ahead, if you like, then store in a single layer in a tightly covered container. About 1 hour before filling or serving, recrisp for 10 minutes in a moderate oven (350°).
9 Store any unbaked pastry in the freezer or refrigerator. To freeze: Wrap tightly in freezer paper or foil, then thaw for an hour before shaping. Plan to use pastry within a month. To store in refrigerator: Wrap in wax paper, foil or transparent wrap. Plan to bake pastry within a week.

●

Strawberry Crème Tartlets
Beneath plump juicy berries there's a rich butterscotch cream. Shells also make perfect holders for chicken or seafood main dishes.
Bake at 450° for 15 minutes, then at 350° for 45 minutes. Makes twelve 3-inch shells

1 *recipe* BASIC FRENCH PASTRY *(recipe precedes)*
  BUTTERSCOTCH CRÈME *(recipe follows)*
6 *cups (3 pints) strawberries, washed and hulled*
  RUBY BERRY GLAZE *(recipe follows)*

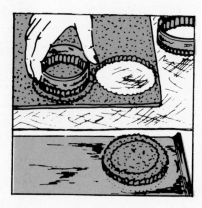

Cut pastry for Strawberry Crème Tartlets into rounds with fluted 3½ inch cutter. Press a 2½ inch cutter into center of each round. Lift cutter out carefully, leaving pastry in place.

1456

Buttery, crispy and light as a wisp—classic French pastry. It's shown here as Strawberry Crème Tartlets.

1 Roll out pastry evenly to a rectangle, about 15x12, on floured pastry cloth. Pastry should be ¼ inch thick. Cut into rounds with fluted or plain 3½-inch cutter. Press a 2½-inch cutter into center of each to bottom, as pictured; lift cutter out carefully, leaving pastry in place. Place rounds on ungreased cookie sheets; chill 30 minutes.
2 Bake in very hot oven (450°) 15 minutes; reduce heat to moderate (350°); bake 15 minutes. Remove pastries from oven. (Leave heat on.) Carefully pry center cutouts loose from shells almost to bottom with small spatula, then lift out and transfer to a second cookie sheet.
3 Bake both shells and centers 30 minutes longer, or until puffed and a rich brown color. Cool on wire racks. (Use centers as bases for canapés, splitting them, if you wish. Or sprinkle with sugar while still hot and serve with fruit or ice cream.)
4 While shells bake, make BUTTERSCOTCH CRÈME. Pick over strawberries, saving about 72 of the smallest and best for shells. Slice remaining (you'll need 1½ cups); make RUBY BERRY GLAZE.
5 To fill shells, spoon 2 tablespoons BUTTERSCOTCH CRÈME into each; top with 6 whole strawberries, standing each tip end up; spoon about 2 tablespoons RUBY BERRY GLAZE over. (Shells may be filled about an hour before serving time, if you like, then chilled.)

Butterscotch Crème
Makes 2 cups

  ¾ cup firmly packed dark brown sugar
  4 tablespoons (½ stick) butter or margarine
  ¼ cup water
  3 tablespoons all-purpose flour
  2 eggs
  1 cup light cream or table cream
  2 teaspoons lemon juice
1½ teaspoons vanilla

1 Combine sugar, butter or margarine and water in top of small double boiler. Heat, stirring constantly, over direct heat, until sugar mixture melts and begins to bubble; simmer 5 minutes. Remove from heat; blend in flour.
2 Beat eggs slightly with cream in small bowl; stir *very slowly* into butter-sugar mixture.
3 Cook over simmering water, stirring constantly, 10 minutes, or until mixture thickens. Cover; continue cooking and stirring often 10 minutes longer. Remove from heat; beat in lemon juice and vanilla until creamy-light with electric or rotary beater; chill.

Strawberry Cheese Tartlets (top) and Almond Twists.

Ruby Berry Glaze
Makes 1½ cups

  ½ cup sugar
  2 tablespoons cornstarch
  ½ cup water
1½ cups sliced, hulled, washed strawberries

1 Combine sugar and cornstarch in small saucepan; slowly stir in water and sliced berries.
2 Cook over low heat, stirring constantly and mashing berries well with back of spoon as they heat, until mixture thickens and boils 3 minutes; cool.

Strawberry Cheese Tartlets
Each two-bites-and-it's-gone dainty hides a rich creamy filling under a rosy berry top.
Bake at 425° for 10 minutes, then at 350° for 20 minutes. Makes 12 tiny tarts

  ½ recipe BASIC FRENCH PASTRY (recipe precedes)
  ½ package (3 or 4 ounces) cream cheese
  ½ cup dairy sour cream
  2 teaspoons granulated sugar
    Dash of pumpkin-pie spice
12 small fresh strawberries, washed and hulled
    10X (confectioners' powdered) sugar

1 Roll out pastry to a ½-inch-thick rectangle, about 11x9, on a lightly floured pastry cloth. Cut out 12 rounds with a fluted or plain 2½-inch cutter, then press a 1½-inch cutter into center of each round, lifting cutter out carefully and leaving pastry in place. Place rounds on a brown-paper-lined cookie sheet; chill 30 minutes.
2 Bake in hot oven (425°) 10 minutes; lower heat to moderate (350°). Bake 20 minutes

1457

longer, or until puffed and richly golden. Cool completely on wire racks. Carefully pry center cutouts loose from shells almost to bottom with the tip of a sharp knife; lift out and set aside to use for canapé bases or another dessert.

3 Soften cream cheese in a small bowl, then beat in sour cream, sugar, and pumpkin-pie spice until fluffy.

4 Spoon into shells, dividing evenly. Dip tips of strawberries in 10X sugar; stand, tip ends up, on top of filling. Chill until serving time.

Almond Cream Horns of Plenty

If you want to make just 12 horns, use only half of the pastry. Then shape the rest into another treat.

Bake at 450° for 15 minutes, then at 350° for 15 minutes. Makes 2 dozen 5-inch horns

 12 sugar ice cream cones
  1 recipe BASIC FRENCH PASTRY (recipe precedes)
    Water
  1 egg, slightly beaten
    Sugar
    ALMOND CREAM (recipe follows)

1 Make your own molds this way: Wrap a 6-inch square of foil around each ice cream cone to cover completely; tuck in foil at top.

2 Divide pastry in half. (Keep one half chilled until you're ready for it.) Roll out evenly to a rectangle, about 21x13, on floured pastry cloth. Pastry should be ⅛ inch thick. Trim all sides to make a rectangle 20x12. Cut pastry lengthwise into 12 strips, each 1 inch wide.

3 Brush with water; wrap each, slightly overlapping, around a foil-covered cone. Start at pointed end and handle carefully so as not to stretch pastry. Place on ungreased cookie sheet; brush with beaten egg; chill 30 minutes.

4 Bake in very hot oven (450°) 15 minutes; reduce heat to moderate (350°); bake 15 minutes longer, or until puffed and a rich brown color.

5 Remove horns from cookie sheet to wire racks; sprinkle with sugar. As each horn is cool enough to handle, carefully remove from mold. Cool completely before filling. Use same molds for baking second half of pastry.

6 Just before serving, fill generously with ALMOND CREAM.

 ALMOND CREAM—Beat 1½ cups cream for whipping, 4 tablespoons 10X (confectioners' powdered) sugar, 1½ teaspoons vanilla and ¾

1458

teaspoon almond extract until stiff in medium-size bowl. Fold in ½ cup ground or very finely chopped blanched almonds. (If cream must stand a little while, cover bowl and chill.) Makes enough to fill 12 horns; double recipe for 24.

Cream Horns Parisienne

This simplified version of puff pastry takes very little time and effort, yet it becomes a most elegant dessert.

Bake at 400° for 20 minutes. Makes 16 five-inch horns

  3 cups sifted all-purpose flour
1½ cups (3 sticks) butter or margarine
  1 cup dairy sour cream
    Water
    Sugar
    PINK CREAM FILLING (recipe follows)

1 Measure flour into a medium-size bowl. Cut in butter or margarine with a pastry blender until mixture is crumbly; add sour cream. Knead lightly with hands just until pastry holds together and leaves side of bowl clean. Wrap dough in wax paper; chill overnight.

2 To make your own cream horn molds: Tear off eight 9-inch pieces heavy-duty foil from an 18-inch-wide roll. Fold each piece in half to make a square; fold square crosswise to make a triangle. Using center of longest side of triangle as tip of cone, start at one side and roll up to form a slim cone.

3 Divide pastry in half. Keep one half refrigerated until ready to use. Roll out evenly to an 18x10-inch rectangle on floured pastry board. Cut pastry lengthwise into 8 strips, each 1¼ inches wide.

4 Moisten each strip lightly with water. Starting at pointed end, wrap around cone-shaped foil, overlapping slightly. Place on ungreased cookie sheet. Chill 30 minutes; brush with water; sprinkle with sugar.

5 Bake in hot oven (400°) 20 minutes, or until puffed and a rich brown color.

6 Remove horns to wire rack to cool. As each horn is cool enough to handle, carefully remove from mold. Cool completely before filling. Use same molds for baking second half of pastry.

7 Fill cones just before serving.

 PINK CREAM FILLING—Beat 2 cups cream for whipping, 2 tablespoons sugar and ½ teaspoon almond extract until stiff in medium-size bowl. Fold in 2 tablespoons finely chopped maraschino cherries and 2 teaspoons syrup from cherries. Add a drop of red food coloring, if you wish. Makes enough to fill 16 horns.

 If you wish to make only 8 horns, use only

Elegant, easy-to-make Almond Cream Horns of Plenty. The filling is simply almond-scented whipped cream.

Cream Horns Parisienne are filled with cherry cream.

½ of filling recipe. Shape second half of horns on molds. Place in a single layer in a pan; freeze. When frozen, wrap in foil or transparent wrap. When ready to use, bake as directed. No need to defrost.

●

Almond Twists
Fluffy cream spills out of each tube of shattery golden pastry.
Bake at 425° for 10 minutes, then at 350° for 20 minutes. Makes 12 twists

½ *recipe* BASIC FRENCH PASTRY *(recipe precedes)*
1 *egg, slightly beaten*
Granulated sugar
1 *cup cream for whipping*
2 *tablespoons 10X (confectioners' powdered) sugar*
1 *teaspoon vanilla*
½ *teaspoon almond extract*

1 Make twist molds this way: Wrap a 4-inch-wide piece of foil around each of 12 wooden clothespins to cover each completely.
2 Roll out pastry to a ¼-inch-thick rectangle, 18x12, on a lightly floured pastry cloth. Cut pastry lengthwise into 12 strips, each 1 inch wide.
3 Wrap each strip, overlapping slightly, around a foil-covered clothespin, handling carefully so as not to stretch pastry; place on brown-paper-lined cookie sheet. Brush pastry with beaten

egg; sprinkle lightly with granulated sugar; chill 30 minutes.
4 Bake in hot oven (425°) 10 minutes; lower heat to moderate (350°). Bake 20 minutes longer, or until puffed and richly golden. While still hot, push out foil-covered clothespins with handle of spoon. Cool twists completely on wire racks before filling.
5 For serving, beat cream with 10X sugar, vanilla and almond extract until stiff in a small bowl. Spoon into twists, working from both ends, to fill. Or fill a pastry bag with cream and squeeze into twists.

Did Napoleon like Napoleons? He certainly would have found these crispy, cream-filled pastries delectable.

Napoleons

Ribbons of pink frosting decorate this golden pastry layered with a creamy vanilla filling.
Bake at 450° for 15 minutes, then at 350° for 45 minutes. Makes 12 individual pastries

1 *recipe* BASIC FRENCH PASTRY *(recipe precedes)*
ROYAL CREAM FILLING *(recipe follows)*
BUTTERY FROSTING *(recipe follows)*

1 Roll out pastry evenly to a rectangle, about 16x10, on floured pastry cloth. Pastry should be ⅜ inch thick. Trim all sides to make a rectangle 15x9. Divide in half lengthwise, then cut each half into 6 even-size blocks. Place on ungreased cookie sheets; prick all over with fork; chill 30 minutes.
2 Bake in very hot oven (450°) 15 minutes; reduce heat to moderate (350°); bake 45 minutes longer, or until puffed and a rich brown color. Cool completely on wire racks.
3 While pastry bakes, make ROYAL CREAM FILLING.
4 When ready to fill, split each pastry rectangle lengthwise into 3 layers; put 2 layers together with ROYAL CREAM FILLING between and on top.
5 Make frosting. Spread white frosting on tops. While it is still soft, drizzle three thin lines of pink frosting crosswise over white from tip of knife, then draw knife in two even lines lengthwise through frostings to make a pattern. Place on top of filled layers. (Layers may be filled and frosted about an hour before serving time, if you like, then chilled.)

Royal Cream Filling
Makes 3 cups

½ *cup sugar*
6 *tablespoons all-purpose flour*
¼ *teaspoon salt*
3 *eggs, slightly beaten*
2 *cups milk*
2 *tablespoons butter or margarine*
1 *teaspoon vanilla*

1 Combine sugar, flour and salt in top of double boiler; gradually blend in eggs and milk.
2 Cook over simmering water, stirring constantly, 10 minutes, or until thickened. Cover; continue cooking, stirring occasionally, 10 minutes longer.
3 Pour into medium-size bowl; stir in butter or margarine until melted, and vanilla; cover; chill.

1460

Buttery Frosting
Makes about ½ cup

1½ cups sifted 10X (confectioners' powdered) sugar
3 tablespoons butter or margarine
2 tablespoons milk
1 teaspoon vanilla
Red food coloring

1 Combine all ingredients except red food coloring in medium-size bowl; beat until creamy-smooth.
2 Spoon about one-fourth of the frosting into a cup; blend in a drop or two of red food coloring to tint a rich pink.

Raspberry Turnovers
Each puffed pocketbook of shattery crisp pastry hides a sweet fruity filling.
Bake at 450° for 15 minutes, then at 350° for 30 minutes. Makes 12 large turnovers

1 recipe BASIC FRENCH PASTRY (recipe precedes)
¾ cup red raspberry jam
1 egg, slightly beaten
Sugar

1 Roll out pastry evenly to a rectangle, about 21x16, on floured pastry cloth. Pastry should be ⅛ inch thick. Trim all sides to make a rectangle 20x15. Cut lengthwise into thirds, then crosswise into quarters to make 12 five-inch squares.
2 Spoon 1 tablespoon raspberry jam into middle of each square; brush edges with beaten egg; fold dough over to make a triangle. Press edges together firmly with thumb to seal; brush top with beaten egg. Place on ungreased cookie sheets; chill 30 minutes.
3 Bake in very hot oven (450°) 15 minutes; reduce heat to moderate (350°); bake 30 minutes longer, or until turnovers are puffed and a rich brown color.
4 Remove *at once* from cookie sheets to wire

Puffy as pillows, the pastry for Raspberry Turnovers. It's the flaky Basic French Pastry used another way.

Making strudel may seem an impossible task. Admittedly, it isn't the easiest recipe. But, it can be made.

1462

racks; sprinkle tops lightly with sugar. Let cool about 10 minutes before serving.

●

Raspberry-Apple Strudel
Bake at 350° for 1 hour. Makes 10 to 12 servings

　3 cups sifted all-purpose flour
　1 egg
　1 cup (2 sticks) butter or margarine, melted
　¾ cup lukewarm water
　1 can (1 pound, 4 ounces) pie-sliced apples
1½ cups fine dry bread crumbs
　1 jar (10 ounces) raspberry preserves
　¼ cup granulated sugar
　¼ teaspoon red food coloring
　　10X (confectioners' powdered) sugar

1 Sift flour onto wax paper.

2 Beat egg in a large bowl; stir in 2 tablespoons of the melted butter or margarine and half of the water. Beat in half of the flour until smooth, then remaining water and remaining flour. (Dough will be slightly elastic.)
3 Lightly oil hands and a pastry board; turn dough out onto board. Knead a few times; shape into a ball. Pick up ball and throw down onto board for 10 minutes, or until dough is very smooth and elastic. Again shape into a ball; place on board; cover with a warm bowl. Let stand 20 minutes.
4 Drain apples and dice, then pat between sheets of paper toweling to remove as much moisture as possible. Combine with ½ cup of the bread crumbs, raspberry preserves, granulated sugar and food coloring in a medium-size bowl; toss lightly to mix.
5 Spread a large tablecloth or folded sheet over

a card table or 3-foot-square kitchen table, leaving at least 6 inches overhang on all sides to hold cloth in place. Keep the table away from the wall so you can move around it as you work. Sprinkle 2 tablespoons flour over cloth and rub in well to keep dough from sticking.

6 Place dough in middle of cloth. Pat into a square, then roll out to an 18-inch square, picking up dough and turning it over several times to prevent sticking. Brush dough lightly with melted butter or margarine.

7 Place hands under middle of dough and, using your fists, back of hands or palms with fingers together, pull and stretch dough toward table edge. Move round and round the table, stretching a little more each time, until dough becomes tissue-thin and hangs over table edges on all sides. Work slowly, pulling steadily and evenly to avoid large tears that cannot be repaired. Trim off any thick edges of dough. Brush generously with melted butter or margarine; sprinkle with remaining 1 cup bread crumbs.

8 Spoon apple mixture in an 18x3-inch strip at one end of dough, slightly in from edge. Using cloth as a guide, pick up opposite half of dough by the corners and fold over filled half. You should now have a double-thick rectangle with filling at one end. (If dough should wrinkle as you fold it, lift top half carefully and smooth it out.)

9 Starting at filled end and again using cloth as a guide, roll up dough tightly, jelly-roll fashion. Place in a jelly-roll pan, 15x10x1. Brush roll well with melted butter or margarine.

10 Bake in moderate oven (350°), brushing every 15 minutes with remaining butter or margarine, 1 hour, or until golden. Cool in pan just until firm; remove to a cutting board. Press 10X sugar through a sieve on top. Cut crosswise into thick slices with a serrated knife and a sawing motion; serve warm or cold.

STEP-BY-STEP TO PERFECT STRUDEL

Be the envy of everyone with our tissue-thin masterpiece, on your very first try! You can—with a bit of time and patience and a look at our how-to's. (1) After mixing the dough, roll it out to an 18-inch square. A cloth-covered card table makes a fine work area. (2) Stretch the rolled-out dough, using your hands with palms up and fingers together, or your fists—whichever is easier for you. Pull from underneath until dough is paper-thin. (3) Sprinkle bread crumbs over dough and spoon on filling (ours is raspberry-apple) in a strip along one end. Pick up dough and cloth together at opposite side and flip dough over filling. (4) Roll dough as you would a jelly roll . . . and it's ready for the oven.

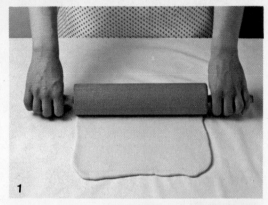

1

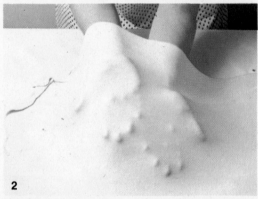

2

3

1463

4

Best Beau Apple Dumplings
Buttery sugar-and-nut-stuffed apple is bundled inside a blanket of rich cheese pastry.
Bake at 425° for 30 minutes. Makes 6 servings

  3 cups sifted all-purpose flour
1½ teaspoons salt
  1 cup vegetable shortening
1½ cups (6 ounces) grated sharp Cheddar cheese
 ⅓ cup water
  4 tablespoons (½ stick) butter or margarine
 ½ cup firmly packed brown sugar
 ½ cup chopped walnuts
  6 small baking apples, pared and cored

1 Sift flour and salt into medium-size bowl; cut in shortening and cheese with pastry blender until mixture is crumbly. Stir in water with a fork, just until dough holds together. Measure out ½ cup and save for making bows in Step 4.
2 Cream butter or margarine with brown sugar in small bowl; add walnuts; stuff mixture into apples.
3 Divide dough into 6 parts; roll out, one part at a time, to an 8-inch square on lightly floured pastry cloth or board. Place a stuffed apple in center; fold pastry up and around fruit; pinch edges to seal; place in baking pan, 13x9x2. Repeat to make 6 dumplings.
4 Roll out saved ½ cup dough to a 6-inch square; cut into 12 strips, each about ½ inch. To make each bow, loop ends of one strip of dough toward middle; fold a second strip over middle.
5 Moisten top of dumpling; put bow in place, pressing down lightly at middle; attach to top of dumpling with wooden picks. Make 12 small rolls of foil, about 1½ inches long, by shaping around handle of wooden spoon; stick through loops so bows will hold their shape while baking.
6 Bake in hot oven (425°) 30 minutes, or until fruit is soft and pastry is golden. (Test fruit with a long, thin metal skewer.)
7 Carefully remove foil rolls by twisting gently to loosen, then take out wooden picks. Serve dumplings warm with cheese, cream, or ice cream.

1465

To cut into a strudel is to see its multi-layer flakiness. The trick is to stretch the pastry tissue-thin.

PERIOD PIECES

**PERIOD PIECES:
OLD-FASHIONED RECIPES
THAT NEVER GO OUT OF
STYLE; MEATS, POULTRY,
VEGETABLES, SALADS,
DESSERTS, CAKES
AND PIES**

America's on a nostalgia kick—old movies on television, old musicals on Broadway, old songs in the air, old clothes on the street (40's fashions are the 70's favorites). The remembrance of things past, of course, includes food, and we're turning once again to those dishes our mothers and grandmothers made, and their mothers and grandmothers before them. There are the robust, rib-sticking roasts and steaks of pioneer days, the bountiful, kind-to-the-budget short ribs and spareribs, the hearty meat loaves and burgers and hotdogs, the crispy fried chicken, the garden-fresh corn-on-the-cob, the bubbling casseroles of potatoes and dried beans, crunchy sweet-sour coleslaw, the kinds of dessert you first cut your sweet tooth on—fruit crisps and cobblers and shortcakes.

One thing *has* changed since the good old days, however. Kitchen time. You can now prepare many of these old-fashioned favorites in record time by using instant seasoners, quick-cooking convenience foods, the magic array of mixes. So, beginning here, an old-fashioned sampler with a streamlined look.

1467

Part of today's nostalgia kick, the old familiar foods.

MEATS

Pioneer Steak-Roast
Makes 4 to 6 servings

1 chuck roast, cut 2 inches thick and weighing
   about 3 pounds
   Instant unseasoned meat tenderizer
1 envelope brown gravy mix
½ cup water
½ cup dry red wine

1 Remove roast from refrigerator an hour before cooking. Sprinkle with tenderizer, following
label directions. Place on grill about 10 inches
above hot coals.
2 Grill, turning once, 50 minutes, or until roast
is as done as you like it. (To test: Cut a small
slit in meat near bone.)
3 While roast cooks, combine gravy mix, water
and wine in a small saucepan; cook, stirring
constantly, until sauce thickens and boils 1
minute.
4 Carve roast into ¼-inch-thick slices; serve
with wine sauce.

Shaker Steaks
Makes 4 servings

4 club steaks, weighing about 12 ounces each
   Freshly ground pepper
4 medium-size tomatoes, sliced thin
   Salt
   Sugar
¼ pound blue cheese, crumbled

1 Sprinkle steaks with pepper; place on grill
about 6 inches above hot coals.
2 Grill 6 minutes; turn; continue grilling 3 minutes.
3 Overlap several tomato slices on top of each
steak; sprinkle with salt, sugar, pepper and blue
cheese. Grill 3 to 4 minutes longer, or until
cheese melts, tomatoes are hot and steaks are
as done as you like them.

Barbecued Short-Ribs Dinner
Makes 4 to 6 servings

4 pounds beef short ribs
1 envelope (about 1½ ounces) spaghetti sauce
   mix
1 teaspoon salt
2 cans (1 pound each) stewed tomatoes
3 cups cooked hot noodles

1 Trim any excess fat from short ribs. Brown,
a few pieces at a time, in a Dutch oven; pour
off all drippings. Return all meat to Dutch oven.
2 Sprinkle spaghetti sauce mix and salt over
ribs; add tomatoes. Stir lightly to mix; heat to
boiling; cover.
3 Simmer 3 hours, or until meat is very tender.
4 Spoon noodles onto a deep large serving
platter; spoon ribs and sauce over top. Sprinkle
with chopped parsley, if you wish.

Baked Stuffed Spareribs
Bake at 450° for 1 hour, then at 400° for 30
minutes. Makes 8 servings

2 racks of spareribs (about 4½ pounds)
1 package (8 ounces) corn-bread stuffing mix
1 tablespoon fennel seeds
1 cup boiling water
1 can (6 ounces) frozen concentrate for
   orange-pineapple juice
1 can (about 9 ounces) crushed pineapple,
   drained
½ cup sugar

1 Place spareribs in a single layer on a rack
in a shallow roasting pan.
2 Bake in very hot oven (450°) 1 hour; remove
from oven. Lower oven temperature to hot
(400°). Pour all drippings from roasting pan.
3 Combine stuffing mix and fennel seeds in a
medium-size bowl; drizzle water over top; toss
until evenly moist.
4 Place 1 side of ribs, curved side up, on rack
in roasting pan; spoon stuffing mixture into
hollow; top with remaining ribs, curved side
down.
5 Mix orange-pineapple concentrate, pineapple
and sugar in a medium-size saucepan; heat
slowly, stirring constantly, to boiling, then simmer, stirring several times, 5 minutes. Spoon
half over ribs.
6 Bake in hot oven (400°) 15 minutes; spoon
remaining fruit mixture over top. Bake 15 minutes longer, or until ribs are tender.

Frankburgers
Makes 6 servings

1 cup catsup
1 tablespoon lemon juice

1 teaspoon seasoned salt
1 teaspoon instant minced onion
1 pound ground beef
1 cup soft bread crumbs (2 slices)
2 teaspoons parsley flakes, crumbled
6 frankfurters
6 frankfurter rolls
½ cup sliced green onions

1 Blend catsup, lemon juice, seasoned salt and onion in a 1-cup measure.
2 Combine ground beef, bread crumbs, parsley flakes and ½ cup of the catsup mixture in a large bowl; mix lightly until well blended. Divide into 6 even mounds.
3 Pat each mound into a rectangle, 6x4, on a sheet of wax paper; top with a frankfurter. Roll up tightly, jelly-roll fashion, using wax paper as a guide; pinch edges to seal. Brush with part of the remaining catsup mixture; place on grill about 6 inches above hot coals.
4 Grill, turning several times and brushing with remaining catsup mixture, 10 minutes, or until frankfurters are hot, and beef is as done as you like it.
5 While meat cooks, toast rolls on side of grill; butter, if you wish. Place each meat roll in a frankfurter roll; sprinkle with green onions.

Western Wieners
Makes 4 servings, 2 sandwiches each

1 large ripe avocado
1 envelope (2 packets) guacamole dip mix
1 large ripe tomato
8 frankfurters
4 split hamburger buns
2 tablespoons butter or margarine

1 Halve avocado; pit and peel. Mash well in a small bowl; stir in dip mix. Peel tomato; seed; stir into avocado mixture. Chill at least an hour to season.
2 Score frankfurters every ¼ inch, cutting not quite through; twist each into a circle; fasten with a wooden pick. Place on grill about 6 inches above hot coals.
3 Grill, turning several times, 10 minutes, or until puffed and heated through.
4 While frankfurters heat, toast buns on side of grill; spread with butter or margarine. Place each frankfurter in a bun; spoon avocado mixture in centers.

POULTRY

Cornmeal-Crusty Fried Chicken
Makes 8 servings

1½ cups yellow cornmeal
  1 envelope Italian salad dressing mix
  ½ cup cream for whipping
  2 broiler-fryers, weighing about 2 pounds each, cut up
    Vegetable oil

1 Combine cornmeal and salad dressing mix on a sheet of wax paper; pour cream into a pie plate.
2 Dip chicken pieces into cream, then roll in cornmeal mixture to coat well; let stand on wire racks about 5 minutes.
3 Pour vegetable oil to a depth of 1 inch into each of 2 large frying pans; heat until a few drops of water sprinkled into oil sizzle. Add chicken and brown slowly, turning several times; cover. Cook 20 minutes longer, or until chicken is tender. Drain on paper toweling. Serve hot.

Pilgrim Turkey Legs
Makes 4 servings

4 turkey drumsticks, weighing about 1 pound each
½ cup (1 stick) butter or margarine
½ cup prepared mustard
1 tablespoon leaf rosemary, crumbled

1 Place drumsticks on grill about 10 inches above hot coals.
2 Melt butter or margarine in a small saucepan; stir in mustard and rosemary. Brush part over turkey.
3 Grill, turning and brushing with more butter mixture every half hour, 2½ hours, or until meat is tender.
Note—If you prefer to cook turkey in oven, follow seasoning directions above. Bake in moderate oven (350°) 2½ hours, or until meat is tender.

1469

VEGETABLES

Indian Corn
Makes 12 servings

12 ears of corn with husks
  PARMESAN BUTTER (recipe follows)
  CHILI BUTTER (recipe follows)

1 Peel back husks from corn, leaving stub on; remove all silk. Spread kernels with part of either PARMESAN BUTTER or CHILI BUTTER.
2 Pull husks back in place; tie tips with string. Place ears on grill about 6 inches above hot coals.
3 Grill, turning often, 25 minutes, or until kernels are tender. Serve with remaining seasoned butter.
Note—To cook corn in oven, prepare, following Steps 1 and 2. Or remove husks and silk, butter ears, and wrap each in a double-thick sheet of foil; place in a large shallow pan. Bake in hot oven (400°), turning often, 25 minutes.
  PARMESAN BUTTER—Blend 1 cup (2 sticks) butter or margarine, ½ cup grated Parmesan cheese, ½ teaspoon crumbled basil and 1 teaspoon salt in a small bowl. Makes about 1¼ cups.
  CHILI BUTTER—Blend 1 cup (2 sticks) butter or margarine and 1 envelope (2 packets) chili-cheese dip mix in a small bowl. Makes about 1 cup.

Colonial Baked Limas
Bake at 400° for 1 hour. Makes 12 servings

4 cans (1 pound each) cooked dried lima beans
½ cup chili sauce
½ cup molasses
1 tablespoon instant minced onion
1 tablespoon prepared mustard
½ cup bacon-flavor bits

1 Combine beans and liquid, chili sauce, molasses, onion and mustard in a 12-cup shallow baking dish; stir lightly to mix.
2 Bake in hot oven (400°) 1 hour, or until beans are brown and bubbly. Stir in bacon bits.
3 Serve in individual bean pots, if you wish. Or, to carry to a picnic, spoon into a large bean pot; cover. Wrap in several thicknesses of newspaper. Beans will stay warm for about 1 hour.

1470

Scalloped Potatoes
Bake at 375° for 1 hour and 20 minutes. Makes 4 to 6 servings

4 medium-size potatoes, pared and sliced thin (4 cups)
1 medium-size onion, peeled and sliced
1 can (10¾ ounces) condensed cream of celery soup
⅓ cup milk
2 tablespoons butter or margarine

1 Parboil potatoes in boiling water in a large saucepan 1 minute; drain well. Place half in a 7-cup baking dish; cover with onion, then remaining potatoes.
2 Blend soup and milk in a small bowl; pour over potato mixture. Dot with butter or margarine; cover.
3 Bake in moderate oven (375°) 1 hour; uncover and bake 1 hour longer until browned and bubbling.

SALADS

Picnic Bean Salad
Makes 6 servings

1 jar (about 8 ounces) sweet mustard pickles
½ cup mayonnaise or salad dressing
½ teaspoon sugar
1 can (1 pound, 4 ounces) white kidney beans, drained
1 can (1 pound) red kidney beans, drained
1½ cups finely chopped celery

1 Drain dressing from pickles into a small bowl. Measure 3 tablespoonfuls and blend with mayonnaise or salad dressing and sugar in a cup.
2 Spoon white beans, red beans and celery in rings on a deep serving platter; pile pickles in center.
3 Just before serving, drizzle dressing over all; toss lightly to mix.

Coleslaw-Tomato Cups
Makes 6 servings

1 small head of cabbage, weighing about 1½ pounds

2 tablespoons sugar
6 medium-size tomatoes
2 tablespoons mayonnaise or salad dressing
2 tablespoons cream
2 tablespoons lemon juice
½ teaspoon salt
  Dash of pepper

1 Quarter cabbage; core; shred fine. Place in a large bowl.
2 Sprinkle sugar over cabbages; toss lightly to mix; cover. Chill at least 30 minutes to crisp.
3 While cabbage chills, cut a thin slice from top of each tomato; scoop out insides. Turn tomato cups upside down in a pie plate to drain; chill.
4 Blend mayonnaise or salad dressing, cream, lemon juice, salt and pepper in a cup.
5 Drain cabbage; drizzle dressing over top. Toss lightly to mix. Spoon into tomato cups. Serve on lettuce-lined salad plates, if you wish.

Tomato-Aspic Crown
Makes 6 servings

2 envelopes unflavored gelatin
3 cups tomato-juice cocktail
1 can (8 ounces) tomato sauce
2 teaspoons Worcestershire sauce
1 large cucumber
½ cup bottled oil-and-vinegar salad dressing
½ teaspoon salt

1 Soften gelatin in 1½ cups of the tomato-juice cocktail in a medium-size saucepan. Heat, stirring constantly, until gelatin dissolves; remove from heat.
2 Stir in remaining tomato-juice cocktail and tomato and Worcestershire sauces. Pour into a 4-cup mold. Chill several hours, or until firm.
3 Slice cucumber thin; place in a shallow dish. Drizzle with dressing; sprinkle with salt; cover. Chill at least an hour to season.
4 When ready to serve, unmold onto a large serving plate.
5 Drain liquid from cucumber. Overlap slices in a ring around salad.

DESSERTS, CAKES AND PIES

Glazed Rice Pudding
Makes 6 servings

¾ cup uncooked regular rice
2 eggs

2½ cups milk
¼ teaspoon ground nutmeg
1 package (about 4 ounces) vanilla pudding and pie filling mix
½ cup orange marmalade
2 nectarines, peeled, pitted and sliced

1 Cook rice, following label directions; set aside.
2 Beat eggs slightly with milk and nutmeg in a small bowl; stir into pudding mix in a medium-size saucepan. Cook, stirring constantly, just until mixture starts to boil.
3 Fold in rice. Spoon into a large shallow serving bowl; chill.
4 Just before serving, melt marmalade in a small saucepan; drizzle part over pudding. Arrange nectarine slices, pinwheel fashion, on top; brush with remaining marmalade.

Raspberry Cream Mold
Makes 8 servings

1 package (6 ounces) raspberry-flavor gelatin
2 cups boiling water
¼ cup lemon juice
1 can (1 pound, 14 ounces) fruit cocktail
½ cup mayonnaise or salad dressing
1 container (4½ ounces) frozen whipped dessert topping, thawed
1 cup tiny marshmallows

1 Dissolve gelatin in boiling water in a large bowl; stir in lemon juice.
2 Drain syrup from fruit cocktail into a cup, then stir syrup into gelatin mixture; beat in mayonnaise or salad dressing.
3 Place bowl in a deep pan of ice and water to speed setting. Chill, stirring several times, until as thick as unbeaten egg white.
4 Stir in whipped topping; fold in marshmallows and fruit cocktail. Spoon into an 8-cup mold. Chill several hours, or overnight, until firm.
5 When ready to serve, unmold onto a serving plate. Frame salad with small lettuce leaves, if you wish.

1471

Apple Crisp
Bake at 350° for 35 minutes. Makes 8 servings

12 zwieback (half a 6-ounce package)
2 cans (1 pound, 4 ounces each) pie-sliced apples

1½ cups firmly packed brown sugar
 1 teaspoon ground cinnamon
 ¼ teaspoon ground nutmeg
 ½ cup (1 stick) butter or margarine, melted
   Cream

1 Crush zwieback coarsely.
2 Combine apples, brown sugar, cinnamon and nutmeg in a large bowl; toss lightly to mix. Spoon about one third of the mixture into a deep 8-cup baking dish. Sprinkle with one third of the zwieback, then drizzle one third of the melted butter or margarine over top. Repeat layers two more times.
3 Bake in moderate oven (350°) 35 minutes, or until bubbly in center. Serve warm or cold with cream.

Strawberry-Orange Shortcake
Bake at 400° for 20 minutes. Makes 12 servings

 2 packages orange muffin mix
   Eggs
   Milk
 4 tablespoons (½ stick) butter or margarine
 1 cup sifted 10X (confectioners' powdered) sugar
1½ cups cream for whipping
 6 cups sweetened sliced strawberries

1 Prepare both packages of muffin mix with eggs and milk, following label directions. Pour into 2 greased 9-inch round layer-cake pans.
2 Bake in hot oven (400°) 20 minutes, or until center springs back when lightly pressed with fingertip.
3 While shortcake bakes, cream butter or margarine with 10X sugar until fluffy and smooth in a small bowl. Beat cream until stiff in a medium-size bowl.
4 Remove shortcake layers from pans; spread each with 10X sugar mixture. (It will melt into shortcake.) Stack layers, with strawberries and whipped cream between and on top, on a deep serving plate. Cut in wedges with a sharp knife; serve warm.
Note—For a smaller family-size shortcake, halve all ingredients, then split layer and put back together with strawberries and whipped cream.

Cherry-Blossom Cobbler
Bake at 400° for 20 minutes. Makes 6 servings

 1 cup granulated sugar
 3 tablespoons cornstarch

 3 cups pitted tart red cherries
1½ cups biscuit mix
 3 tablespoons cinnamon-sugar
 ½ cup cream for whipping
 4 tablespoons (½ stick) butter or margarine, melted
 ¼ cup finely chopped walnuts

1 Mix granulated sugar and cornstarch in a medium-size saucepan; stir in cherries. Cook slowly, stirring constantly, until mixture thickens and boils 3 minutes. Spoon into a deep 6-cup baking dish; place in oven to keep hot while fixing biscuit topping.
2 Combine biscuit mix, 1 tablespoon of the cinnamon-sugar, cream and 2 tablespoons of the melted butter or margarine in a medium-size bowl; stir just until mixture is moist.
3 Turn dough out onto a lightly floured pastry cloth or board; knead gently ½ minute. Roll out to a rectangle, 12x6. Brush with remaining 2 tablespoons melted butter or margarine; sprinkle with remaining 2 tablespoons cinnamon-sugar and walnuts. Starting at a long side, roll up, jelly-roll fashion; cut into 1-inch slices. Arrange over hot cherry filling.
4 Bake in hot oven (400°) 20 minutes, or until topping is golden and filling bubbles up. Serve warm with cream, if you wish.

Yankee Blueberry Pie
Bake at 400° for 45 minutes. Makes one 9-inch pie

 4 cups (2 pints) blueberries, washed and stemmed
 1 cup sugar (for filling)
 3 tablespoons quick-cooking tapioca
 ¼ teaspoon salt
 ¼ teaspoon ground cinnamon
 1 package piecrust mix
 2 tablespoons butter or margarine
 2 tablespoons sugar (for glaze)
 1 teaspoon lemon juice

1 Place blueberries in a large bowl; sprinkle with the 1 cup sugar, tapioca, salt and cinnamon; toss lightly to mix.
2 Prepare piecrust mix, following label directions, or make pastry from your favorite two-crust recipe. Roll out half to a 12-inch round on a lightly floured pastry cloth or board; fit into a 9-inch pie plate; trim overhang to ½ inch.
3 Spoon fruit mixture into shell; dot with butter or margarine.

Old favorites, new treatment: Strawberry-Orange Shortcake, Yankee Blueberry Pie and Toasted Coconut Cake.

4 Roll out remaining pastry to an 11-inch round; cut out three leaf shapes near center with a 1½-inch-long cookie cutter to let steam escape. (Save cutouts.) Place crust over filled shell. Trim overhang to ½ inch; turn edges under, flush with rim; flute edge. Moisten one side of cutouts with water; press between holes onto top of pastry.
5 Mix the 2 tablespoons sugar and lemon juice in a cup; brush over crust.
6 Bake in hot oven (400°) 45 minutes, or until pastry is golden and juices bubble up. Cool on a wire rack. Serve plain or with lemon sherbet, if you wish.

Toasted Coconut Cake
Bake at 360° for 30 minutes. Makes one 9-inch double-layer cake

    1 package white cake mix
    2 eggs, separated
1⅓ cups water
    1 teaspoon vanilla
    1 can (3½ ounces) flaked coconut LEMON-EGG
      FILLING (recipe follows)
    1 package fluffy white frosting mix
      Boiling water

1 Prepare cake mix with egg whites, water and vanilla, following label directions. Pour into two greased and floured 9x1½-inch round layer-cake pans.
2 Bake in moderate oven (350°) 30 minutes, or until centers spring back when lightly pressed with fingertip. Cool in pans on wire racks 10 minutes. Loosen around edges with a knife; turn out onto racks; cool completely.
3 Spread coconut in a shallow pan; heat in same oven, shaking pan several times to mix, 5 minutes, or until toasted. Set aside until ready to frost cake.
4 Make LEMON-EGG FILLING; chill.
5 When ready to finish cake, put layers together, with LEMON-EGG FILLING between, on a large serving plate.
6 Prepare frosting mix with boiling water, following label directions. Spread on side and top of cake; pat toasted coconut over all.
LEMON-EGG FILLING—Mix ½ cup sugar, 2 tablespoons cornstarch and a dash of salt in a small saucepan; stir in ⅔ cup water. Cook over medium heat, stirring constantly, until mixture thickens and boils 3 minutes. Beat 2 egg yolks (from cake) in a small bowl; stir in about half of the hot mixture, then stir back into saucepan. Continue cooking, stirring constantly, 2 minutes (do not boil); remove from heat. Stir in 2 tablespoons lemon juice and 1 teaspoon butter or margarine. Chill.

1473

Two oven-fresh apple pies, one open face (Swiss Apple Tart), one closed. Also, Pumpkin-Apple Pie-ettes.

PIES THEY'LL APPLAUD

**PIES THEY'LL APPLAUD:
THE MAKING OF PIES—INSTANT AND
OLD-FASHIONED, FRUIT PIES,
CUSTARD AND CREAM PIES,
MERINGUE PIES, CHIFFON PIES,
CHEESE PIES, ICE CREAM,
ANGEL AND OTHER SPECIALTY PIES**

Is there *anyone* who doesn't dote upon pie? Who doesn't enjoy tucking into a tart apple pie blanketed with flaky-golden crust, or into a billowing too-good-to-be-true chocolate chiffon pie, a sky-high lemon or coconut meringue pie, a silky-rich cheese pie glazed with cherries or berries, a spicy-velvety pumpkin pie?

The list of pies goes on and on. To simplify the recipe repertoire, we've divided the pies into six basic types; *fruit pies,* some of them double-crusted, others open face in the Continental manner . . . *cream and custard pies* . . . *meringue pies* (meringue-topped, that is—fillings are usually of the cream or custard type) . . . *chiffon pies* (a fairly modern hybrid of cream and meringue pies made by folding the meringue into the cream filling) . . . *cheese pies* (cool, smooth and, sadly, caloric) . . . and, finally, *specialty pies,* which include the meringue-crusted *angel pies* and *ice cream pies* (their fillings are ice cream, literally).

You'll find a handsome selection of them all in the pages that follow, also recipes for pastry, crumb, nut-and cookie-dough crusts plus tips for making decorative edgings and toppings. These, truly, are pies the whole family will applaud.

THE MAKING OF PIES— INSTANT AND OLD-FASHIONED

Most cooks feel great pride in serving home-made pie created with half a dozen or so basic ingredients. But this takes time and skill. If you're short on both or either, buy crusts, fillings and toppings partly or fully prepared. Or, for the ultimate in convenience, rely on ready-to-serve bakery or frozen pies. Whichever you buy is up to you, but remember that you can choose from more than three dozen ingredients and often two to four brands of each, all varying widely in price. To get the most for your money, consider these facts.

PIE TAKES CRUST

Pie bakers claim that it's a snap to stir up pastry from flour, shortening, salt and water. But even within the two major ingredients, there are differences worth noting.

Flour—Here you'll find three kinds; All-purpose,

1475

1476

self-rising and instant. All-purpose is just what its name implies and makes a tender flaky crust. Self-rising starts as all-purpose flour, but has leavening and salt added by the miller. It makes a mealy crust, rather than one that's flaky. Instant flour, specially processed to pour freely, usually requires more shortening and liquid than the other types, so it's best to follow the recipe recommended by the manufacturer. All varieties come in 2- to 10-pound (or larger) containers. and because prices stay remarkably steady, there's no particular advantage in stocking up.
Shortening—According to the dictionary, all fats are shortening. But as we know them today, fats for making pastry include lard, oils and a specific product labeled SHORTENING.

Lard is the forerunner of all, comes from the fat of pigs and has long been preferred by many experienced pastry makers for its great ''shortening'' power. You'll find 1-pound cartons as well as larger containers and pails, but even in the pound size, it will be your thriftiest buy.

Oils rate tops in convenience, as they can be mixed and measured easily. Most are made from corn, soybeans, cottonseed, peanuts or safflower seeds. Usually supermarkets carry several brands in pint, quart or larger containers. A cooking reminder: Always follow a recipe that specifically calls for oil.

Shortenings, smooth and creamy-white or yellow, differ according to whether they're made of animal or vegetable fat or the two combined. All come in 1- or 3-pound cans and keep well, so it pays to buy the largest size you can use within a reasonable length of time. For even greater savings, keep your eye on sales.
Shortcut crusts—Here you can choose from packaged piecrust mixes in dry or stick form—that cost only a penny or two more than does making your own crust; frozen crusts rolled and neatly fitted into baking pans; or crumb crusts that come three ways—as cereals or cookies to crush yourself, as packaged crumbs or, easiest of all, as prepared crusts in foil pans. When figuring the cost of any of these, be sure to count your savings in time.

FILLINGS: UNLIMITED VARIETY

Fruit —This list reads like a pie lover's dream, as choices are almost endless the year round.

Fresh, canned, frozen and dried fruits have long shared great popularity. In fresh fruits, apples and bananas, especially, know no sea-

son; others come and go from late spring through early fall. Older families recall the goodness of pies made from dried apples, apricots, peaches, prunes or raisins, and these favorites still rate big displays on grocery shelves in a variety of cartons or transparent bags. As far as work is concerned, they need only brief simmering before mixing with other filling ingredients.

Ready-for-the-shell canned pie fillings are relative newcomers, but how we take them for granted! All are processed from special varieties of fruits to preserve their fresh flavor and bright color. Fruits are first cooked with just the right amount of sugar, extract, spices, flavorings and thickening, then canned, ready for your cupboard shelf. Popular flavors include apple, cherry, blueberry, peach, pineapple, strawberry and raisin. (Not to be overlooked are canned prepared mincemeat, pumpkin and lemon fillings.) When you consider their quality and the fussing that's been done for you (peeling, cutting and pitting), plus the other ingredients that have been added, you'll certainly agree that their price is attractive.
Cream—For many cooks it isn't particularly hard to combine milk (whole, evaporated, sweetened condensed, skim or nonfat), eggs, sugar and flavorings into a velvety cream filling, but it does take a bit of watchful cooking. More economical than homemade recipes are packaged pudding and pie filling mixes in more than a half dozen luscious flavors. Some are instant and just need to be whipped up with milk in a bowl; others need some cooking.

For the easiest fillings you ever ''cooked,'' just open a can of prepared pudding. Available in a variety of flavors, all brands are creamy-rich and ready to spoon from can to crust. Most cost considerably less than do home recipes.

THE CROWNING GLORY
A pouf of old-fashioned cream that you whip yourself, a generous squeeze of cream from a pressurized can or a spoonful of frozen whipped topping from a plastic container finishes any pie with a professional flourish. Or you can depend on the handy packaged topping mixes to do the same job with only a slight assist from you.

Plain Pastry I
Recipe makes enough for a 9-inch single-crust pie

1¼ cups sifted all-purpose flour
1 teaspoon salt

½ cup shortening
3 to 4 tablespoons cold water

1 Sift flour and salt into a medium-size bowl; cut in shortening with a pastry blender until mixture is crumbly.
2 Sprinkle water over, a tablespoon at a time; mix lightly with a fork just until pastry holds together and leaves side of bowl clean.

Plain Pastry II

Recipe makes enough for a 9-inch lattice-top or double-crust pie

2 cups sifted all-purpose flour
1 teaspoon salt
⅔ cup shortening
3 to 4 tablespoons cold water

1 Sift flour and salt into a medium-size bowl; cut in shortening with a pastry blender until mixture is crumbly.

2 Sprinkle water over, a tablespoon at a time; mix lightly with a fork just until pastry holds together and leaves side of bowl clean.

Skinny Piecrust

429 calories (single 8'' piecrust with pastry cut-outs). Conventional recipe, 1,045 calories.

½ cup sifted all-purpose flour
¼ cup diet margarine
¼ teaspoon salt
¼ teaspoon baking powder

1 Have diet margarine *room temperature* (this is important).
2 Sift flour, salt and baking powder together in a deep bowl.
3 Add margarine all at once. Cut in with fork or pastry blender and continue mixing until no pastry sticks to the sides of the bowl.
4 Shape into a ball. Wrap in wax paper and refrigerate until *thoroughly chilled* (one hour or more).

HOW TO ROLL PASTRY

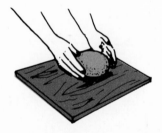

1 To roll pastry to an even round, form into a ball, flatten with hand then start rolling from the center to the outside all around. Your pastry will be even and uniformly thick.

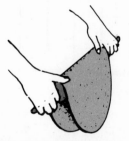

2 To handle that flaky pastry you have just rolled out, roll the dough up and over your rolling pin. Then lift from the pastry board to the pie plate and gently unroll it into place.

HOW TO MAKE A SUNBURST DESIGN

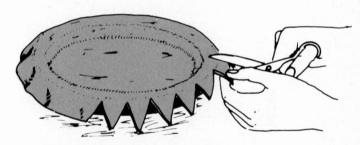

Frame the inviting filling with a different—and gay—edging. Here's how: Fit the bottom crust into pie plate, leaving an overhang of 1½ inches. With scissors to speed up the job, snip even saw-tooth cuts all around and fold edge over filling toward center.

1477

PIES THEY'LL APPLAUD

HOW TO FRAME PIES WITH DECORATIVE EDGES

Start with a Stand-Up Collar:

Flute —To make this easy trim, press right forefinger along inside of rim between thumb and forefinger on outside. Repeat about every inch.

Rope—A wooden skewer—or a slim pencil—is your handy helper here. Press it, twisting slightly, diagonally into pastry all around edge to make even, widely spaced ridges.

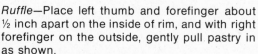

Ruffle—Place left thumb and forefinger about ½ inch apart on the inside of rim, and with right forefinger on the outside, gently pull pastry in as shown.

Start with a Flat Edge:

Double scallop—No talent needed for this simple design, but how it dresses up a pie! To make it, press tip of a teaspoon into the pastry rim in two even rows.

Button—Use your sewing thimble to cut dainty pastry rounds, then place them, just touching, around rim (moisten it first) and poke holes with a skewer.

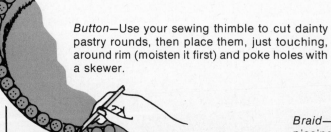

Braid—Cut thin pastry strips; braid each three, piecing enough together to go around pie plate. Brush pastry rim with water; press braid on top.

HOW TO MAKE A LATTICE TOP PIE

Weave a lattice top this way: First lay half of the pastry strips evenly across top of filled pie. Handle carefully to avoid stretching or tearing dough. Then weave the first cross strip, over and under, through center, and each time you add another, fold back every other right-angle strip.

FRUIT PIES

Favorite Apple Pie
A bit of cream makes the generous filling taste so much richer.
Bake at 400° for 1 hour. Makes one 9-inch pie.

1 recipe PLAIN PASTRY II (recipe precedes)
¾ cup granulated sugar
¼ cup firmly packed brown sugar
2 tablespoons all-purpose flour
½ teaspoon ground cinnamon
¼ teaspoon ground nutmeg
⅛ teaspoon salt
6 cups thinly sliced pared tart apples (about 2 pounds)
¼ cup cream
3 tablespoons butter or margarine
1 tablespoon milk

1 Prepare PLAIN PASTRY II. Roll out half to a 12-inch round on a lightly floured pastry cloth or board; fit into a 9-inch pie plate. Trim overhang to ½ inch.
2 Mix granulated and brown sugars, flour, spices and salt in a small bowl. Spread about one third of the apples into prepared pastry shell; sprinkle with one third of the seasoning mixture. Repeat layering two more times with remaining apples and seasoning mixture. Pour cream into center; dot with butter or margarine.

3 Roll out remaining pastry to an 11-inch round; cut several slits near center to let steam escape; cover pie. Trim overhang to ½ inch; turn edges under, flush with rim; flute edge. Brush top with milk and sprinkle lightly with granulated sugar, if you wish.
4 Bake in hot oven (400°) 1 hour, or until pastry is golden and juices bubble up. Cool at least an hour on a wire rack. Serve plain or with ice cream.

Cinnamon-Apple Pie
Bake at 400° for 35 minutes. Makes one 9-inch pie

2 cans (1 pound, 4 ounces each) pie-sliced apples
⅔ cup sugar (for filling)
¼ cup cornstarch
¼ cup red cinnamon candies
1 tablespoons butter or margarine
1 package piecrust mix
Milk
Sugar (for topping)

1 Drain liquid from apples into a cup; place apples in a large bowl.
2 Mix ⅓ cup of the sugar and cornstarch in a small saucepan; stir in ⅓ cup of the apple liquid, cinnamon candies and butter or margarine. Cook slowly, stirring constantly, until candies melt and mixture thickens and boils 3 minutes. Stir in remaining ⅓ cup sugar; pour over apples; cool.
3 Prepare piecrust mix, following label directions, or make pastry from your favorite double-crust recipe. Roll out half to a 12-inch round on a lightly floured pastry cloth or board; fit into a 9-inch pie plate. Trim overhang to ½ inch. Spoon apple mixture into crust.
4 Roll out remaining pastry to an 11-inch round; cut a round or fancy shape from center with a 1½-inch cookie cutter; place over filling. Trim overhang to ½ inch; turn edges under, flush with rim; flute to make a stand-up edge.
5 Cut 8 leaf shapes from pastry trimmings with a cookie cutter. Moisten one side of each with water; arrange evenly around cutout on top of pie. Brush top crust with milk; sprinkle with sugar.
6 Bake in hot oven (400°) 35 minutes, or until pastry is golden. Cool pie completely on a wire rack.

1479

PIES THEY'LL APPLAUD

Double Apple Pie
Bake at 400° for 45 minutes. Makes one 9-inch pie

2 cups cider
1 package piecrust mix
4 medium-size tart cooking apples, pared, quartered, cored and thinly sliced
1 cup firmly packed light brown sugar
¼ cup sifted all-purpose flour
1 teaspoon apple pie spice
1 teaspoon grated lemon peel
⅛ teaspoon salt
2 tablespoons butter or margarine
1 tablespoon milk
2 teaspoons granulated sugar
1 package (6 ounces) cubed Cheddar cheese

1 Boil cider rapidly in a small saucepan until reduced to ½ cup (this will take about 10 minutes); cool.
2 Prepare piecrust mix, following label directions, or make pastry from your own favorite two-crust recipe. Roll out half to a 12-inch round on a lightly floured pastry cloth or board; fit into a 9-inch pie plate; trim overhang to ½ inch.
3 Combine apples, brown sugar, flour, spice, lemon peel and salt in a large bowl, tossing to coat apple slices evenly. Spoon into pie shell, arranging evenly; dot with butter or margarine.
4 Roll out remaining pastry to an 11-inch round; cut strips, ½ inch wide, with a pastry wheel or sharp knife. Weave strips on top of pie to make crisscross top crust; trim ends of strips. Moisten edge of bottom crust; press ends of strips onto

There are apple pies and apple pies. Two extra-decorative ones: Double Apple (left), Apple Crown Tart.

bottom crust; flute to make a stand-up edge. Brush strips with milk; sprinkle granulated sugar over top. Carefully pour cider into center of pie.

5 Bake in hot oven (400°) 45 minutes, or until filling bubbles; remove from oven. Place cubes of cheese in spaces of lattice top.

6 Return to oven for 3 minutes, or just until cheese is melted. Cool on wire rack. For best flavor, serve slightly warm.

Nutty and crunchy praline-topped Apple Candy Pie.

Swiss Apple Tart

Apple slices, asparkle with a sugary topping, float in a sweet custard base. It's a bit fussy to make, but so worth the effort!

Bake at 400° for 40 minutes. Makes one 10-inch pie

    1 package piecrust mix
      OR: 1 recipe PLAIN PASTRY II (recipe pre-
      cedes)
      Whole cloves
    4 medium-size apples, pared, quartered,
      cored and sliced thin
    ½ cup sugar (for filling)
    1 tablespoon lemon juice
    3 eggs
    1½ cups cream for whipping
    2 tablespoons butter or margarine, melted
    ¼ teaspoon ground nutmeg
    2 tablespoons sugar (for topping)

1 Prepare piecrust mix, following label directions, or make PLAIN PASTRY II.

2 Roll out about ⅔ to a 14-inch round on a lightly floured pastry cloth or board; fit into a 10-inch pie plate. Trim overhang to ¼ inch; press pastry under edge of rim of pie plate to prevent shrinking if you wish to make the fancy "flower" edge. Or trim overhang to ½ inch; turn under, flush with rim; flute to make a stand-up edge.

3 To make "flower" rim, roll out remaining pastry and trimmings ¼ inch thick; cut out about 20 "flowers" with a truffle cutter or a tiny cookie cutter. Or cut out plain rounds with the half teaspoon of a measuring-spoon set.

4 Moisten rim of pastry shell with water; lay cutouts, ½ inch apart, around rim; press with fingertip, then stick a whole clove through base of each cutout to hold in place.

5 Combine sliced apples, ½ cup sugar and lemon juice in a medium-size bowl; toss to mix. Arrange slices, overlapping, in a circle in bottom of prepared shell.

6 Bake in hot oven (400°) 20 minutes.

7 Beat eggs slightly in a 4-cup measure; stir in cream, melted butter or margarine and nutmeg; pour over apples.

8 Continue baking 10 minutes; sprinkle with the

2 tablespoons sugar. Bake 10 minutes longer, or until top is golden. Cool on wire rack at least 2 hours before cutting.

Apple Candy Pie

Favorite of many boasts a new melt-in-your-mouth flavor when topped with a rich praline "frosting."

Bake at 400° for 55 minutes. Makes one 9-inch pie

    1 package piecrust mix
    6 cups thinly sliced, pared, tart apples
    ¾ cup granulated sugar
    4 tablespoons all-purpose flour
    ½ teaspoon ground mace
    ¼ teaspoon salt
    6 tablespoons (¾ stick) butter or margarine
    2 tablespoons lemon juice
    ½ cup firmly packed brown sugar
    2 tablespoons cream
    ½ cup chopped pecans

1481

1 Prepare piecrust mix, following label directions, or make your favorite double-crust recipe. Roll out half to a 12-inch round on a lightly floured pastry cloth or board; fit into a 9-inch pie plate; trim overhang to ½ inch.

2 Combine sliced apples with granulated sugar, flour, mace and salt in a large bowl; toss lightly to mix; spoon into prepared pastry shell. Dot with 2 tablespoons of the butter or margarine and sprinkle with lemon juice. (Set remaining butter or margarine aside for topping.)

3 Roll out remaining pastry to an 11-inch round; cut several slits near center to let steam escape; cover pie. Trim overhang to ½ inch; turn edges under, flush with rim; flute to make a stand-up edge.

4 Bake in hot oven (400°) 50 minutes, or until pastry is golden and juices bubble up; remove from oven.

5 Melt remaining 4 tablespoons butter or margarine in a small saucepan; stir in brown sugar and cream. Heat slowly to boiling; remove from heat; stir in pecans. Spread over top of pie; return to oven.

6 Bake 5 minutes longer, or until topping bubbles and crust is richly glazed. Cool on a wire rack at least an hour before cutting.

Apple Cream-Crumble Pie

Cream makes a rich custardlike layer for this apple favorite; mellow cheese curlicues, its golden topknot.

Bake at 425° for 1 hour. Makes one 9-inch pie

    1 stick piecrust mix (2 to a package)
    5 large baking apples (about 3 pounds)
    2 tablespoons lemon juice
    ½ cup sugar (for filling)
    2 tablespoons all-purpose flour (for filling)
    ½ teaspoon ground nutmeg
    ½ cup sugar (for topping)
    ½ cup sifted all-purpose flour (for topping)
    ½ cup (1 stick) butter or margarine
    1 cup cream for whipping
    ¼ pound (half an 8-ounce package) unsliced
        process American cheese, chilled

1 Prepare piecrust mix, following label directions, or make pastry from your own favorite recipe. Roll out to a 12-inch round on lightly floured pastry cloth or board; fit into a 9-inch pie plate; trim overhang to ½ inch; turn under flush with rim; flute.

2 Pare, quarter and core apples, then halve each quarter crosswise. (You should have about 7 cups.) Place in large bowl; sprinkle lemon juice over.

3 Mix ½ cup sugar, 2 tablespoons flour and nutmeg in cup; sprinkle over apples, tossing to coat well; spoon into prepared shell.

4 Combine ½ cup sugar and ½ cup flour in small bowl; cut in butter or margarine with pastry blender until crumbly; sprinkle over apples. Cover pie loosely with foil; place on large cookie sheet for easy handling.

5 Bake in hot oven (425°) 45 minutes; uncover;

1482

drizzle ½ cup cream over; bake 15 minutes longer, or until top is golden. Remove pie from oven and place on wire rack. Drizzle remaining ½ cup cream over; cool about 1 hour, or until filling is set.

6 Serve plain, or with cheese curls. To make: Shave cheese into thin strips with a vegetable parer, pulling parer towards you; roll each around fingertip to curl; chill. Pile on top of pie just before serving.

Apple Crown Tart

Bake at 375° for 20 minutes. Makes one 8-inch pie

    1½ cups sifted all-purpose flour
    ¼ cup sugar
    ¼ teaspoon salt
    ⅓ cup cold butter or margarine
    1 egg yolk
    4 teaspoons water
    3 medium-size red eating apples
    1 jar (10 ounces) apple jelly
    ¼ cup water
    2 teaspoons lemon juice
    1 package (3½ ounces) lemon-flavor whipped
        dessert mix
    ½ cup cold milk
        Pistachio nuts, chopped

1 Combine flour, sugar and salt in a medium-size bowl; cut in butter or margarine with a pastry blender until mixture resembles cornmeal; beat egg yolk with the 4 teaspoons water; pour over flour mixture; knead with hands.

2 Shape ⅓ of the dough into a 4-inch circle; shape remaining dough into a roll about 4 inches long and 1 inch in diameter. Wrap each portion of dough in plastic wrap; chill 1 hour.

3 Roll out circle of dough to an 8-inch round; trim to fit the bottom of an 8x1½-inch round cake pan with removable bottom. (If cake pan does not have a removable bottom, fold two long lengths of foil into 2-inch-wide strips. Crisscross on bottom of pan. Use as lifters when crust cools.)

4 Cut roll of dough into 20 slices; overlap the slices around the inside edge of the lined cake pan, pressing lightly to seal to dough at base; fit a piece of aluminum foil into pan; fill with dry beans or rice, to keep dough flat and smooth.

5 Bake in moderate oven (375°) 10 minutes; remove foil and beans or rice; prick bottom with a fork; bake 10 minutes longer, or until lightly browned. Cool on a wire rack; remove side of cake pan, then loosen pastry shell from base of pan and slide onto a serving plate.

6 Pare, core and quarter apples; cut into ⅛-inch

Two favorite fruit pies in new guise: Apple Pie-Cakes with fluffy Cheddar topping and cinnamon stick garnish and behind, French Peach Tart with golden peaches spiraling around a quick vanilla pudding filling.

slices; melt apple jelly with the ¼ cup water and lemon juice in a large skillet; stir in apple slices; cover; poach about 5 minutes, or until tender. Remove apples to a medium-size bowl with a slotted spoon. Refrigerate about 1 hour, or until thoroughly chilled. Reserve cooking liquid.

7 When apples have chilled, combine dessert mix with milk in a small bowl; beat at medium speed 1 minute; gradually beat in 1 cup chilled apple slices; continue beating for 2 minutes; spoon mixture into baked shell. Chill 1 hour.

8 Arrange remaining apple slices, overlapping, around edge of tart over filling, leaving a small open space in the center. Cook reserved apple-jelly mixture over low heat, stirring constantly, 5 minutes, or until slightly thickened; cool. Spoon over apple slices to glaze. Sprinkle nuts in space in center.

●

Apple Pie-Cakes

Filling is a deep layer of chilled spicy fruit and the topping, crisp pastry and a Cheddar-rich puff.

Bake pastry at 400° for 15 minutes. Makes 8 servings

1 cup sugar
4 tablespoons cornstarch
1 teaspoon ground cinnamon
½ cup water
2 cans (1 pound, 4 ounces each) pie-sliced
  apples
2 tablespoons butter or margarine
1 teaspoon lemon juice
1 recipe PLAIN PASTRY I (recipe precedes)
  CHEDDAR FLUFF (recipe follows)

1 Blend sugar, cornstarch and cinnamon in a large saucepan; stir in water and apples. Cook, stirring constantly, until mixture thickens and boils 3 minutes.
2 Stir in butter or margarine and lemon juice; spoon into a baking dish, 8x8x2. Chill at least 2 hours, or until set enough to cut neatly.
3 While apple mixture chills, prepare PLAIN PASTRY I or use ½ package piecrust mix, following label directions. Roll out to an about-9-inch square on a lightly floured pastry cloth or board; trim edges with a knife or pastry wheel to make an 8-inch square. Halve crosswise, then cut each in quarters lengthwise to make 8 pieces in all. Place on a cookie sheet; prick several times with a fork; brush lightly with milk and sprinkle with sugar, if you wish.
4 Bake in hot oven (400°) 15 minutes, or until golden. Cool on cookie sheet on a wire rack.
5 When ready to serve, cut apple mixture in half crosswise, then in quarters lengthwise; lift onto serving plates with a pancake turner. Top each with a piece of pastry and a spoonful of CHEDDAR FLUFF; garnish with a cinnamon stick, if you wish.

CHEDDAR FLUFF—Combine 1 cup grated Cheddar cheese (4 ounces) and 1 package (3 or 4 ounces) cream cheese in a medium-size bowl; beat until fluffy-light. (This spread keeps well in the refrigerator, but should be served at room temperature for best flavor.) Makes about 1 cup.

1484

French Peach Tart
Glazed peach slices whirl atop a rich creamy layer in golden pastry for this show-off—but see how easy to make!
Bake shell at 425° for 15 minutes. Makes one 9-inch tart

1 recipe PLAIN PASTRY I (recipe precedes)
1 package (about 4 ounces) vanilla-flavor instant pudding mix
1 cup milk
1 cup (8-ounce carton) dairy sour cream
¼ teaspoon almond extract
1 can (1 pound, 14 ounces) cling peach slices
1 tablespoon cornstarch
1 tablespoon lemon juice
¼ cup flaked coconut

1 Prepare pastry, following recipe, or use ½ package piecrust mix, following label directions. Roll out to a 12-inch round on a lightly floured pastry cloth or board; fit into a 9-inch pie plate. Trim overhang to ½ inch; turn under, flush with rim; flute to make a stand-up edge. Prick shell all over with a fork.
2 Bake in hot oven (425°) 15 minutes, or until golden; cool completely on a wire rack.
3 Combine pudding mix with milk, sour cream and almond extract in a medium-size bowl; prepare, following label directions; pour into cooled crust. Let stand at room temperature 5 minutes, or until set.
4 Drain syrup from peaches into a 2-cup measure. Cut any thick peach slices in half lengthwise, then arrange all, slightly overlapping, on top of pudding.
5 Blend ⅔ cup of the peach syrup slowly into cornstarch in a small saucepan. (Save any remaining syrup to sweeten a fruit beverage.) Cook, stirring constantly, until mixture thickens and boils 3 minutes; stir in lemon juice. Cool slightly, then spoon over peaches to glaze; chill. Just before serving, garnish pie with cone of coconut.

●

Jumbo Fruit Tart
Bake shell at 375° for 15 minutes. Makes 8 servings

2 cups sifted all-purpose flour
¼ cup sugar
½ cup (1 stick) butter or margarine
1 egg, slightly beaten
2 packages vanilla-flavor whipped-dessert mix
  Milk
  Water
1 can (about 9 ounces) sliced pineapple, drained
½ cup blueberries, washed and stemmed
1 can (about 1 pound) apricot halves, drained
3 medium-size firm ripe bananas
  Lemon juice
1 jar (10 ounces) apple jelly

1 Sift flour and sugar into a medium-size bowl; cut in butter or margarine with a pastry blender until mixture is crumbly. Stir in egg, then knead pastry in bowl until smooth. Press over bottom and up side of a 14-inch pizza pan; flute edge. Prick shell well all over with a fork.

2 Bake in moderate oven (375°) 15 minutes, or until golden. Cool completely in pan on a wire rack.
3 Prepare whipped-dessert mix with milk and water, following label directions. Chill 20 minutes, or until mixture mounds on a spoon. Spread evenly in pastry shell; chill until set.
4 Place one pineapple slice in center of filling; halve remaining slices; place in a circle around whole one. Fill in spaces around pineapple with blueberries. Place apricot halves, hollow side up, next to pineapple.
5 Peel bananas; slice diagonally; brush with lemon juice to prevent darkening. Place around apricots on filling.
6 Heat jelly until melted in a small saucepan; cool slightly. Spoon over fruits. Chill until serving time. Cut in wedges.

Apricot Sour Cream Pie
Golden raisins and toasty almonds go with the apricots to turn an old favorite into a different pie treat.
Bake at 450° for 10 minutes, then at 350° for 30 minutes. Makes one 9-inch pie

 1 stick piecrust mix (2 to a package)
    OR: 1 recipe PLAIN PASTRY I (recipe precedes)
 2 eggs
 1 cup sugar

Who says pizza has to be tomato? This one's peach.

 ¼ teaspoon salt
 ⅛ teaspoon ground ginger
 1 cup dairy sour cream
 ½ cup golden raisins
 ½ cup diced dried apricots
 ½ cup toasted slivered almonds (from a 5-ounce can)
 1 tablespoon lemon juice
 ¼ teaspoon almond extract

1 Prepare piecrust mix, following label directions, or make PLAIN PASTRY I.
2 Roll out to a 12-inch round on a lightly floured pastry cloth or board; fit into a 9-inch pie plate. Trim overhang to ½ inch; turn under, flush with rim; flute to make a stand-up edge.
3 Beat eggs slightly in a medium-size bowl; beat in sugar, salt and ginger until well blended. Stir in remaining ingredients; pour into prepared shell.
4 Bake in very hot oven (450°) 10 minutes; lower heat to moderate (350°). Bake 30 minutes longer, or until center is set and pastry is golden. Cool on wire rack.

Peach Pizza
Makes 6 to 8 servings

 1 package (8 ounces) cream cheese
 ½ cup (1 stick) butter or margarine
 1 cup sifted all-purpose flour
 2 tablespoons sugar
 2 tablespoons milk
 1 can (1 pound, 5 ounces) peach pie filling

1 Divide block of cream cheese in half. Blend one half with butter or margarine until smooth in a medium-size bowl; stir in flour to make a soft dough. Chill 30 minutes, or until firm enough to handle.
2 Roll out dough to a 13-inch round on a lightly floured pastry board; fit into a 12-inch pizza pan, pressing firmly to edge. Prick dough all over with a fork.
3 Bake in hot oven (400°) 15 minutes, or until golden. Cool in pan on wire rack.
4 Combine remaining half of cream cheese with sugar and milk in a small bowl; beat until smooth. Spread over prepared crust; top with peach pie filling. Chill at least 10 minutes. Cut in wedges.

Upside-Down Pear Pie
Bake at 375° for 1 hour and 10 minutes. Makes one 9-inch pie

 6 firm ripe pears, pared, quartered, cored and sliced

1485

1¼ cups sugar (for filling)
½ teaspoon ground cinnamon
6 tablespoons (¾ stick) butter or margarine
1 cup sifted all-purpose flour
2 tablespoons sugar (for pastry)
¼ teaspoon salt
2 tablespoons shortening
3 tablespoons cold water

1 Place pears in a large bowl; sprinkle ¼ cup of the sugar and cinnamon over top; toss lightly to mix. Melt 3 tablespoons of the butter or margarine in a saucepan.
2 Sprinkle ¼ cup of the remaining sugar over bottom of a generously buttered deep 9-inch pie plate. Top with one third of the pear slices, 1 tablespoon of the melted butter or margarine and ¼ cup sugar; repeat to make two more layers of each.
3 Sift flour, the 2 tablespoons sugar and salt into a medium-size bowl; cut in remaining 3 tablespoons butter or margarine and shortening with a pastry blender until mixture is crumbly. Sprinkle cold water over top, 1 tablespoon at a time; mix lightly with a fork until pastry leaves side of bowl clean.
4 Roll out on a lightly floured pastry cloth or board to a 9-inch round; cut several slits near center to let steam escape. Place over filling, tucking edges down around pears.
5 Bake in moderate oven (375°) 1 hour and 10 minutes, or until pears are tender and pastry is golden. Cool on a wire rack 5 minutes; invert onto a deep serving platter. Let stand 5 minutes, then lift off pie plate. Cut in wedges; serve warm with cream, if you wish.

Double Fruit Tarts
Each golden pastry shell holds a filling of mellow pears and tart cranberries.
Bake at 375° about 40 minutes. Makes 8 tarts

SOUR CREAM PASTRY (recipe follows)
3 cups washed fresh cranberries
2 large ripe pears
1 cup sugar
2 eggs
¼ cup sifted all-purpose flour
¼ teaspoon salt
⅔ cup dairy sour cream

1 Make SOUR CREAM PASTRY. Roll out about a third at a time, on lightly floured pastry cloth or board; cut into 6-inch rounds, using a saucer for pattern. Fit into 4-inch tart-shell pans or 1-cup glass baking dishes; flute edges. Repeat to make 8 shells.

2 Chop or cut up cranberries; place in medium-size bowl. Pare, halve, core and dice pears; mix with cranberries and ½ cup sugar.
3 Beat eggs in medium-size bowl; stir in remaining ½ cup sugar, flour, salt and sour cream.
4 Fill shells with cranberry-pear mixture; spoon custard mixture over. Place on large cookie sheet or in shallow baking pan for easy handling.
5 Bake in moderate oven (375°) about 40 minutes, or just until custard is set. Cool on wire rack.

SOUR CREAM PASTRY—Sift 2 cups sifted all-purpose flour and 1 teaspoon salt into medium-size bowl; cut in ½ cup shortening with pastry blender until mixture is crumbly. Blend in ⅓ cup dairy sour cream. Sprinkle about 2 tablespoons ice water over; mix quickly with pastry blender, or 2 knives, until dough clings together in a ball and leaves side of bowl clean. Makes 8 four-inch tart shells.

Plum Dumpling Pie
Whole plums in a star-shape pastry jacket make this pie look like a king-size dumpling.
Bake at 400° for 45 minutes. Makes one 9-inch pie

2 pounds red plums
2 cups sugar
⅓ cup quick-cooking tapioca
1 teaspoon pumpkin-pie spice
1 package piecrust mix
ORANGE HARD SAUCE (recipe follows)

1 Make pattern for star design (directions follow).
2 Wash plums; cut a slit in one side with sharp knife; remove pits. Toss plums with sugar, tapioca and pumpkin-pie spice in medium-size bowl; set aside while making pastry.
3 Prepare piecrust mix, following label directions, or make pastry from your own favorite 2-crust recipe. Roll out to a 20-inch round on lightly floured pastry cloth or board. Lay star pattern on top, then cut out with pastry wheel.
4 Lay pastry star over rolling pin and transfer to a deep 9-inch pie plate; ease pastry into pie plate, pressing firmly against bottom and side; let points of star hang over edge.
5 Spoon plum mixture into shell; lift points of star up over fruit to middle; turn back tips of points. Place on a cookie sheet to catch any syrup that may cook out.
6 Bake in hot oven (400°) 45 minutes, or until plums are tender and crust is golden.
7 Cool completely on wire rack before cutting. Serve plain or with ORANGE HARD SAUCE.

ORANGE HARD SAUCE—Cream 2 tablespoons

1486

A harvest of fruit pies: Plum Dumpling Pie (behind), Double Fruit Tarts (left), Apple Cream-Crumble Pie.

butter or margarine with ¾ cup sifted 10X (confectioners' powdered) sugar in small bowl; beat in 1 tablespoon orange juice and ½ teaspoon grated orange peel until fluffy. Makes ½ cup.

How to make a 6-point star design:

Cut a piece of brown paper slightly larger than a 20-inch square; mark approximate center with an X. Next, make a 10-inch pencil-string "compass" this way: Tie string to a pencil, then cut string to 10 inches. Holding string end tightly on center X, draw a 20-inch circle. Now divide and mark circle into six equal parts, starting at any point and using the same 10-inch compass as your measured guide. With ruler, join every other mark to make two triangles. (Lines will cross to make a 6-point star.) Cut out star and place pattern on rolled-out pastry.

Harvest Plum Pie

It's tart and juicy and ever so good served warm with big scoops of ice cream.
Bake at 450° for 10 minutes, then at 350° for 40 minutes.
Makes one 9-inch pie

1 package piecrust mix
  OR: 1 recipe PLAIN PASTRY II (recipe precedes)
1¾ cups sugar
½ cup sifted all-purpose flour
½ teaspoon ground cinnamon
¼ teaspoon ground nutmeg
⅛ teaspoon salt
1 teaspoon grated lemon peel
4 cups quartered, pitted plums (2½ pounds)
2 tablespoons butter or margarine

1 Prepare piecrust mix, following label directions, or make PLAIN PASTRY II.
2 Roll out half to a 12-inch round on a lightly floured pastry cloth or board; fit into a 9-inch pie plate; trim overhang to ½ inch.
3 Mix sugar, flour, cinnamon, nutmeg, salt and lemon peel in a small bowl; sprinkle 2 tablespoons over bottom of prepared shell.
4 Top with about a quarter of the plums; sprinkle with about ½ cup sugar mixture. Repeat with remaining plums and sugar mixture to make 3 more layers of each; dot with butter or margarine.
5 Roll out remaining pastry to an 11-inch round; cut several slits near center to let steam escape; cover pie. Trim overhang to ½ inch; turn under, flush with rim; flute. (If you wish to form the ropelike edge, make even ridges around rim by pressing a pencil diagonally into pastry.)
6 Bake in very hot oven (450°) 10 minutes; lower heat to moderate (350°). Bake 40 minutes

longer, or until juices bubble up and pastry is golden. Cool on wire rack.

Crisscross Cherry Pie

Nutmeg makes this popular treat just that much better.
Bake at 400° for 40 minutes. Makes one 9-inch pie

1 PLAIN PASTRY II (recipe precedes)
2 cans (about 1 pound, 6 ounces each) cherry-pie filling
½ teaspoon ground nutmeg
2 tablespoons melted butter or margarine

1 Prepare pastry. Roll out half to a 12-inch round; fit into a 9-inch pie plate; trim overhang to ½ inch.
2 Combine remaining ingredients in a large bowl; spoon into shell.
3 Roll out remaining pastry to a rectangle, 12x8; cut lengthwise into 10 strips. Weave strips over filling to make a crisscross top; trim overhang to ½ inch; turn under, flush with rim; flute edge.
4 Bake in hot oven (400°) 40 minutes, or until pastry is golden and juices bubble up. Cool completely on a wire rack before cutting.

Cherry-Berry Pie

Bake crust at 375° for 8 minutes. Makes one 9-inch pie

1 package coconut cream pie mix
½ cup chopped pecans
3 tablespoons sugar
⅓ cup butter or margarine, softened
3 cups cold milk
1 can (1 pound, 5 ounces) blueberry pie filling
1 can (1 pound, 5 ounces) cherry pie filling
½ teaspoon vanilla

1 Combine graham crumbs (from mix package) with pecans and sugar in a medium-size bowl; blend in butter or margarine. Press mixture firmly over bottom and side of a 9-inch pie plate.
2 Bake in moderate oven (375°) 8 minutes, or until set; cool completely in pie plate on a wire rack, then chill thoroughly.
3 Prepare filling mix with 2½ cups of the milk, following label directions; pour into prepared crust. Chill at least 15 minutes, or until firm.
4 Drain as much sauce as possible from blueberry and cherry pie fillings and set aside for ice cream or custard toppings another day. Spoon blueberry mixture around edge on pie; spoon cherry mixture in center; chill.
5 Just before serving, prepare topping mix with remaining ½ cup milk and vanilla, following label

Crisscross Cherry Pie is a culinary classic. It's shown here two ways, unadorned and à la mode, with a hefty scoop of vanilla ice cream plumked on top.

Very patriotic-looking Cherry Berry Pie. Wreaths of blueberries and red cherries float on creamy coconut custard filling.

directions. Spoon part in center of pie; serve remainder separately.

Little Blueberry Pie

Perfect for a twosome. Cheese-rich pastry makes enough for a bonus pie shell or four tart shells.

Bake at 425° for 30 minutes. Makes one 6-inch pie

    1 cup sifted all-purpose flour
    ½ teaspoon salt
    ¼ cup shortening
    1 package (3 or 4 ounces) cream cheese
    2 tablespoons water
    1 cup blueberry-pie filling (from an about-1-
        pound, 6-ounce can)

1 Sift flour and salt together; cut in shortening and cream cheese until mixture is crumbly. Sprinkle water over; mix lightly just until pastry holds together.

2 Divide into thirds; roll out one to an 8-inch round. Fit into a 6-inch pie plate; trim overhang to ½ inch.

3 Spoon blueberry-pie filling into shell. Roll out another third of pastry to a 7-inch round; cut slits near center to let steam escape; cover pie. Trim overhang to ½ inch; fold under, flush with rim; flute all around edge to seal.

4 Bake in hot oven (425°) 30 minutes, or until pastry is golden and juices bubble up.

Note—Bake remaining third of pastry as a 6-inch pie shell, or make into 4 tart shells this way: Divide pastry in quarters; roll out each to a 5-inch round. Fit into 3-inch tart-shell pans; trim any overhang; prick well. Bake in hot oven (425°) 15 minutes, or until golden. Fill with remaining blueberry-pie filling and top with a dollop of whipped cream or dairy sour cream for another dessert treat. If you prefer to make one big pie for 4 to 6 servings, fit half of pastry into an 8-inch pie plate, spoon in 1 can (about 1 pound, 6 ounces) blueberry-pie filling and cover with remaining pastry. Bake in hot oven (425°) 40 minutes, or until golden.

1490

Tasty tabletop of pies—fruit pies under lattice crusts, under fancily cut-out crusts, under plain old-fashioned crusts. A rich pumpkin pie garlanded with peach slices, a super-rich pecan pie and a fluffy, chocolate-trimmed chiffon pie are here, too.

Deep-Dish Blueberry Pie

Add a dash of cinnamon to cream for a delightful topping for this old-timer.
Bake at 400° for 25 minutes. Makes 6 servings

    4 cups blueberries, washed and drained
    ¾ cup sugar
    2 tablespoons all-purpose flour
    2 tablespoons butter or margarine
    1 stick piecrust mix (2 to a package)
    ½ cup cream for whipping
      Cinnamon and sugar

1 Place berries in 4-cup baking dish; sprinkle mixture of sugar and flour over; toss to coat berries; dot with butter or margarine.
2 Prepare piecrust mix, following label directions, or make pastry from your own favorite recipe. Roll out to shape of baking dish; cut several slits near center to allow steam to escape; place over fruit; press edge with fork to seal.
3 Bake in hot oven (400°) 25 minutes, or until golden-brown and juices bubble up; cool on wire rack.
4 Beat cream until stiff in small bowl; spoon on top of pie; sprinkle lightly with cinnamon and sugar.

Cranberry-Peach Pie

Bake at 400° for 45 minutes. Makes one 9-inch pie

    ¾ cup sugar
    2 tablespoons all-purpose flour
    1 teaspoon grated lemon peel
    ¼ teaspoon ground cinnamon
    2 cans (about 1 pound each) sliced cling peaches, drained
    2 cups fresh cranberries, washed and stemmed
    1 package piecrust mix
    1 egg, well beaten
    ½ cup 10X (confectioners' powdered) sugar
    2 teaspoons water

1 Mix sugar, flour, lemon peel and cinnamon in a medium-size bowl; add peaches and cranberries. Toss lightly to coat fruit.
2 Prepare piecrust mix, following label directions, or make pastry from your favorite double-crust recipe. Roll out half to a 12-inch round on a lightly floured pastry cloth or board; fit into a 9-inch pie plate; trim overhang to ½ inch. Spoon cranberry-peach mixture into prepared pastry shell.
3 Roll out remaining pastry to an 11-inch round; cut a fancy design or several slits near center to let steam escape; cover pie. Trim overhang to ½ inch; turn edges under, flush with rim; flute to make a stand-up edge.
4 Mix egg with 1 tablespoon water in a small bowl; brush over pastry for a rich glaze when baked.
5 Bake in hot oven (400°) 45 minutes, or until top is golden-brown and juices bubble up. Cool on a wire rack.
6 While pie is still warm, mix 10X sugar with water until smooth in a small bowl. Drizzle over pie.

Cranberry Petal Pie

A real beauty! Sweet pears form the petal trim atop a mellow two-fruit filling.
Bake at 450° for 10 minutes, then at 350° for 30 minutes. Makes one 9-inch pie

    3 cups fresh cranberries
    1 can (8 ounces) crushed pineapple
    1½ cups sugar
    1 recipe PLAIN PASTRY I (recipe precedes)
    ¼ cup chopped walnuts (from a 5-ounce can)
    3 tablespoons all-purpose flour
    ¼ teaspoon salt
    ¼ teaspoon ground cinnamon
    1 can (1 pound) pear halves, well drained
    1 tablespoon butter or margarine, melted

1 Combine cranberries, pineapple and syrup and sugar in a medium-size saucepan; cook, stirring constantly, just until sugar dissolves and cranberries start to pop. Pour into a medium-size bowl; let stand until cool.
2 Prepare pastry, following the recipe or use ½ package piecrust mix, following label directions. Roll out to a 12-inch round on a lightly

1492

Cranberry-Peach Pie drizzled while warm with glaze.

floured pastry cloth or board; fit into a 9-inch pie plate. Trim overhang to ½ inch; turn under, flush with rim; flute to make a stand-up edge.

3 Mix walnuts with flour, salt and cinnamon in a cup; stir into cooled cranberry mixture; spoon into shell.

4 Arrange pear halves, rounded sides up, spoke fashion on top. (If you wish to make a fluted pears edging, make 4 even curved cuts lengthwise, ⅛ inch deep, in each pear half with a sharp thin-blade knife. [Work carefully, as pears are soft.] Make a second curved cut just behind each line, slanting knife slightly, then lift out the narrow strip of pear.) Pick out 9 walnut halves from remaining in can, if you wish, and place between pears and in center. Brush pears and walnut halves, if using, with melted butter or margarine.

5 Bake in very hot oven (450°) 10 minutes; lower heat to moderate (350°). Bake 30 minutes longer, or until pastry is golden and juices bubble up. Cool completely before cutting.

Cranberry Petal Pie ringed with fluted pear halves.

Gooseberry Fool Pie
An old-fashioned puddinglike dessert inspired this delectable treat.
Bake shell at 325° for 10 minutes. Makes one 9-inch pie

- 1 package (5 ounces) shortbread cookies
- 1 can (about 4 ounces) flaked coconut
- 4 tablespoons (½ stick) butter or margarine, melted
- 4 cups (1 quart) gooseberries
- 1½ cups sugar
- ½ cup water
  Green and yellow food colorings
- 2 cups cream for whipping

1 Crush cookies fine. (There should be 1½ cups crumbs. Tip to speed the job: Place cookies in a transparent bag and roll with a rolling pin.)

2 Measure ¼ cup of the coconut into a shallow pan, then mix remaining with cookie crumbs in a medium-size bowl; blend in melted butter or margarine. Press evenly over bottom and around side of a 9-inch pie plate.

3 Bake in slow oven (325°) 10 minutes, or until set; cool completely on a wire rack. While shell bakes, toast coconut in pan in same oven 5 minutes, or just until golden. Set aside for topping.

4 Wash gooseberries; remove stems and blossom ends. Combine gooseberries with sugar and water in a large saucepan. Heat, stirring constantly, to boiling, then cook, uncovered, 15 minutes, or until berries are tender. Press through a sieve into a medium-size bowl, discarding seeds. Stir in a drop or two each of green and yellow food colorings to tint lime green; chill.

5 Beat cream until stiff in a large bowl; fold in chilled gooseberry mixture until no streaks of green remain; spoon into cooled shell. Sprinkle with toasted coconut. Chill several hours, or until firm.

Autumn Currant Pie
It's sweet—really sweet—but worth every calorie-packed forkful.

PIES THEY'LL APPLAUD

Bake at 425° for 10 minutes, then at 350° for 30 minutes. Makes one 9-inch pie

1 package piecrust mix
2 eggs
2 cups firmly packed brown sugar
2 tablespoons cider vinegar
1 teaspoon vanilla
½ cup (1 stick) butter or margarine, melted
1 cup currants
½ cup chopped walnuts

1 Prepare piecrust mix, following label directions; roll out half to an 11-inch round on lightly floured pastry cloth or board; fit into a 9-inch pie plate; trim flush with rim.
2 Roll out remaining pastry to ⅛-inch thickness. Make a cardboard pattern of a 1-inch-long leaf; cut out 44 pastry leaves with tip of knife; draw leaf veins on each with knife tip.
3 Moisten rim of pastry shell with water; lay about 32 leaves overlapping on rim, pressing each with fingertip to hold in place; put remaining 12 leaves in a pie plate to bake in Step 5.
4 Beat eggs slightly in medium-size bowl; beat in sugar, vinegar and vanilla; stir in remaining ingredients; pour into prepared pastry shell.
5 Bake in hot oven (425°) 10 minutes; reduce heat to moderate (350°); bake 30 minutes longer, or just until firm in center. Put extra leaves in to bake 5 minutes before pie is done. Cool pie on wire rack; arrange baked leaves on top.
6 To serve, cut into 12 wedges, as pie is very rich.

Raspberry-Pear Pie

Bake at 400° for 1 hour. Makes one 9-inch pie

6 large fresh pears
1 tablespoon lemon juice
1 package (10 ounces) frozen red raspberries, thawed
1 cup sugar
½ cup sifted all-purpose flour
¼ teaspoon ground cinnamon
1 package piecrust mix
3 tablespoons butter or margarine

1 Pare pears; quarter, core and slice thin into a large bowl. Drizzle lemon juice over top, then toss to coat well; add raspberries and syrup.
2 Mix sugar, flour and cinnamon in a small bowl; sprinkle over fruit mixture; toss to mix well.
3 Prepare piecrust mix, following label directions, or make pastry from your favorite double-crust recipe. Roll out half to a 13-inch round on a lightly floured pastry cloth or board; fit into a deep 9-inch pie plate; trim overhang to ½ inch. Spoon fruit mixture into crust; dot with the butter or margarine.
4 Roll out remaining pastry to an 11-inch round; cut several slits near center to let steam escape; place over filling. Trim overhang to ½ inch; turn edges under, flush with rim; flute to make a stand-up edge. (If you wish to make a rope edge on pie, turn overhang under, flush with rim, then pinch to make a stand-up edge. Press a pencil or skewer diagonally into stand-up edge all the way around to make wide, evenly spaced ridges.)

Underneath Strawberry Nectar Pie's topping of fresh strawberries lies a smooth pureed apricot filling.

Little pies with big appeal: Glazed Ruby Tartlets. Underneath the jewel-like strawberry glaze lies a cool and satiny-rich filling made of cream cheese.

5 Bake pie in hot oven (400°) 1 hour, or until juices bubble up and pastry is golden. Cool several hours on a wire rack. Garnish with several raspberries and huckleberry leaves, if you wish.

Note—To fix raspberries for garnish, thaw package of fruit called for in recipe just enough to pick out several pretty whole berries. Stand them, not touching, in a small pan; refreeze until time to garnish pie.

Strawberry - Nectar Pie

Strawberries blend with apricots for the unusual flavor in this two-layer treat.

Bake at 425° for 15 minutes. Makes one 9-inch pie

> Pastry for a 9-inch single-crust pie
> 1 can (1 pound, 14 ounces) peeled whole apricots
> ¼ cup sugar
> ¼ cup cornstarch
> ½ teaspoon salt
> 1 teaspoon lemon juice
> Red food coloring
> 4 cups (2 pints) strawberries, washed and hulled

1 Make pastry with piecrust mix, following label directions, or use your own favorite one-crust recipe. Roll out to a 12-inch round on a lightly floured pastry cloth or board; fit into a 9-inch pie plate. Trim overhang to ½ inch; turn under, flush with rim; flute to make a stand-up edge. Prick shell well all over with a fork.

2 Bake in hot oven (425°) 15 minutes, or until golden; cool completely on a wire rack.

3 Drain syrup from apricots into a small bowl; set aside for Steps 4 and 6. Pit apricots; place apricots in an electric-blender container; cover. Beat at high speed 1 minute, or until smooth. (Or press through a sieve into a small bowl.)

4 Combine sugar, cornstarch and salt in a medium-size saucepan; stir in apricot purée and ¼ cup of the saved apricot syrup.

5 Cook, stirring constantly, until mixture thickens and boils 3 minutes; remove from heat. Stir in lemon juice and a few drops red food coloring to tint a bright pink. Cool 30 minutes.

6 Measure 2 tablespoonfuls into a cup and stir in ¼ cup of the saved apricot syrup from Step 3. Set aside for Step 8.

7 Wash, hull and halve 2 cups (1 pint) of the strawberries; stir into remaining cooled apricot mixture. Spoon into baked pastry shell.

8 Wash and hull remaining 2 cups of strawberries. Save one berry for garnish; halve others lengthwise and arrange, cut side down, in an even layer on top of pie. Spoon apricot mixture from Step 6 over; garnish with the saved whole berry. Serve with PINK WHIPPED CREAM, if you wish.

Note—To make PINK WHIPPED CREAM, add a drop or two red food coloring to cream; beat until stiff.

1495

Glazed Ruby Tartlets

Each strawberry is a glistening jewel in a crown of golden pastry.

Bake at 425° for 10 minutes. Makes 6 tarts

Tart Shells

1½ cups sifted all-purpose flour
  2 tablespoons sugar

6 tablespoons (¾ stick) butter or margarine
1 egg
1 tablespoon cold water

Strawberry Glaze

3 cups (from 2 pints) strawberries, washed and hulled
½ cup sugar
2 tablespoons cornstarch
⅛ teaspoon salt
½ cup water

Cream-Cheese Layer

1 package (3 or 4 ounces) cream cheese
2 tablespoons 10X (confectioners' powdered) sugar
1 tablespoon cream for whipping

1 Make tart shells: Sift flour and sugar into medium-size bowl; cut in butter or margarine with pastry blender until mixture is crumbly.
2 Beat egg slightly with water in a cup; sprinkle over flour mixture. Mix lightly with a fork until well blended. Turn out onto wax paper; press into a ball.
3 Roll out half of pastry to ⅛-inch thickness on lightly floured pastry cloth or board; cut out three 6-inch rounds. Fit into three 4-inch tart-shell pans, pressing dough firmly against bottoms and sides; prick all over with a fork. Repeat with remaining pastry to make a total of 6 shells.
4 Bake in hot oven (425°) 10 minutes; cool completely on wire rack before removing from pans. (Tart shells can be made ahead, if you wish.)
5 Make strawberry glaze: Pick over and hull strawberries, saving out 30 of the firmest and prettiest for Step 7. Combine sugar, cornstarch and salt in medium-size saucepan; slowly stir in water and remaining berries. Cook over low heat, stirring constantly and mashing berries as they heat, until mixture thickens and boils 3 minutes. Remove from heat; cool slightly.
6 Make cream-cheese layer: Blend all ingredients in a small bowl until mixture is easy to spread.
7 Spread cheese mixture evenly over bottoms of tart shells; fill with saved whole strawberries, standing each tip end up. Spoon cooled strawberry glaze over each; chill 1 hour, or until set.

1496

Strawberry-Orange Pie

Tart orange peel accents the fruit so pleasingly in this berry-time splurge.
Bake at 425° for 40 minutes. Makes one 9-inch pie

1 package piecrust mix
1⅓ cups sugar
3 tablespoons cornstarch
1 teaspoon grated orange peel
⅛ teaspoon salt
2 pints strawberries, washed, hulled and sliced
2 tablespoons butter or margarine

1 Prepare piecrust mix, following label directions. Roll out half to a 12-inch round; fit into a 9-inch pie plate.
2 Mix sugar, cornstarch, orange peel and salt in a large bowl; stir in strawberries; spoon into shell. Dot with butter or margarine.
3 Roll out remaining pastry; cut several slits near center to let steam escape; cover pie. Trim overhang to ½ inch; turn under, flush with rim; flute.
4 Bake in hot oven (425°) 40 minutes, or until pastry is golden and juice bubbles up. Cool completely before cutting.

Strawberry-Rhubarb Pie

Smidgen of nutmeg is just the right touch for this double-fruit winner.
Bake at 400° for 50 minutes. Makes one 9-inch pie

PLAIN PASTRY II (recipe precedes)
1 pound rhubarb
1 pint strawberries (2 cups)
1¼ cups sugar
5 tablespoons all-purpose flour
¼ teaspoon ground nutmeg
2 tablespoons butter or margarine

1 Make PLAIN PASTRY II. Roll out half to a 12-inch round on a lightly floured pastry cloth or board; fit into a 9-inch pie plate; trim overhang to ½ inch.
2 Wash rhubarb, trim ends and cut into 1-inch pieces. (There should be about 3 cups.) Wash strawberries, hull and halve.
3 Combine rhubarb and strawberries in a medium-size bowl; sprinkle with sugar, flour and nutmeg; toss lightly to mix. Spoon into prepared shell; dot with butter or margarine.
4 Roll out remaining pastry to a rectangle, 12x8; cut lengthwise into 10 strips; weave strips over filling to make a crisscross top. Trim overhang to ½ inch; turn under with bottom crust, flush with rim; flute to make a high stand-up edge.
5 Bake in hot oven (400°) 50 minutes, or until

pastry is golden and juices bubble up. Cool completely on a wire rack before cutting. Serve plain or with ice cream, if you wish.

Mincemeat-Pear Pie

Bake at 400° for 45 minutes. Makes one 9-inch pie

½ *package piecrust mix*
1 *large lemon*
3 *large fresh pears*
1 *jar (1 pound, 12 ounces) prepared mince-meat*
¾ *cup sifted all-purpose flour*
¼ *cup sugar*
½ *teaspoon pumpkin-pie spice*
¼ *cup (½ stick) butter or margarine*

1 Prepare piecrust mix, following label directions, or make pastry from your favorite single-crust recipe. Roll out to a 12-inch round on a lightly floured pastry cloth or board; fit into a 9-inch pie plate. Trim overhang to ½ inch; turn under, flush with rim; flute to make a stand-up edge.
2 Grate 1 teaspoon lemon peel; reserve. Squeeze lemon; measure 2 tablespoons juice; reserve.
3 Pare pears; quarter and core. Slice 1 of the pears into wedges in a small bowl; sprinkle lemon juice over top, then toss lightly to coat well. Chop remaining pears finely.

4 Combine chopped pears, lemon peel, mincemeat and ¼ cup of the flour in a medium-size bowl. Spoon into prepared pastry shell. Arrange pear wedges on top, pinwheel fashion.
5 Combine remaining ½ cup flour, sugar, and pumpkin-pie spice in a small bowl. Cut in butteror margarine with a pastry blender or two knives until mixture is crumbly. Sprinkle crumbs over top of pie.
6 Bake in hot oven (400°) 45 minutes, or until crumbs are golden-brown and filling is bubbly. Cool completely on a wire rack.
7 Garnish with a lemon rose, if you wish. Choose a medium-size lemon and, starting at the stem end, pare off peel in one continuous long strip. Rewind spiral, following natural curl. Stand on stem end; curl spiral as tight as you wish to resemble opened rose.

Duxbury Mince Pie

Bake at 400° for 40 minutes. Makes one 9-inch pie

2 *cups cranberries, washed and stemmed*
1 *cup sugar*
¼ *cup water*
1 *can (1 pound, 6 ounces) mincemeat pie fill-ing*
1 *package piecrust mix*

1 Combine cranberries with sugar and water in a medium-size saucepan. Heat, stirring con-

1497

Mincemeat-Pear Pie, a unique combination of flavors with a spicy streusel topping and lemon rose garnish.

stantly, to boiling; simmer, stirring often, 5 minutes; remove from heat. Stir in pie filling; cool.

2 Prepare piecrust mix, following label directions, or make pastry from your favorite double-crust recipe. Roll out half to a 12-inch round on a lightly floured pastry cloth or board; fit into a 9-inch pie plate; trim overhang to ½ inch. Spoon cranberry mixture into crust.

3 Roll out remaining pastry to a rectangle, 10x8; cut lengthwise into 10 strips. Weave strips over filling to make a crisscross top. Press edges together; turn under, flush with rim; flute to make a stand-up edge. Brush top lightly with milk and sprinkle with sugar, if you wish.

4 Bake in hot oven (400°) 40 minutes, or until juices bubble up and pastry is golden. Cool completely on a wire rack.

●

Mince-Pear Tartlets
Bake at 400° for 40 minutes. Makes 12 tarts

1 package piecrust mix
2 large ripe pears, pared, halved, cored and diced (2 cups)
1⅓ cups prepared mincemeat (from a 1-pound, 12-ounce jar)
2 tablespoons sugar
1 tablespoon all-purpose flour
2 tablespoons Curaçao
Milk
Yellow and green decorating sugars

1 Prepare piecrust mix, following label directions, or make pastry from your favorite double-crust recipe.

2 Roll out half, ⅛ inch thick, on a lightly floured pastry cloth or board. Cut into 4½-inch rounds with a knife or pastry wheel; fit into 3-inch tart-shell pans or large muffin-pan cups. Repeat with remaining half of dough, rerolling trimmings, to make 12 shells in all.

3 Combine pears, mincemeat, sugar, flour and

1498

Another mixture of pear and mincemeat, this one in individual size Mince-Pear Tartlets. To decorate, pastry pear cut-outs colored with green sugar.

Curaçao in a large bowl; toss lightly to mix. Spoon into pastry-lined pans, dividing evenly. Set pans in a jelly-roll pan for easy handling.

4 Cut out 12 small pear shapes from pastry trimmings with a cookie cutter, or cut around your own cardboard pattern with a sharp knife. Place on a cookie sheet; brush very lightly with milk. Mix yellow and green sugars in a cup; sprinkle lightly over cutouts.

5 Bake tarts in hot oven (400°) 40 minutes, or until pastry is golden and juices bubble up. Bake cutouts in same oven 10 minutes, or until lightly golden.

6 Cool tarts in pans on wire racks 5 minutes; loosen carefully at edges with the tip of a small knife. Cool 5 minutes longer; remove from pans to racks. Just before serving, top each with a pastry cutout.

Raisin Cream Pie

Plan on 8 servings with this pie—it's lusciously rich!

Bake at 425° for 40 minutes. Makes one 9-inch pie

    1 package piecrust mix
    3 cups seedless raisins
    1 cup water
    ¾ cup firmly packed brown sugar
    2 teaspoons cornstarch
    ½ teaspoon salt
    2 teaspoons lemon peel
    2 teaspoons lemon juice
    ½ cup chopped walnuts
    1 cup dairy sour cream

1 Prepare piecrust, following label directions; roll out half and line a 9-inch pie plate.

2 Simmer raisins in water 5 minutes; stir in brown sugar, cornstarch and salt, mixed; cook, stirring constantly, 5 minutes.

3 Remove from heat; stir in lemon peel and juice, walnuts and sour cream; spoon into pie shell; cover, crisscross fashion, with ½-inch-wide pastry strips cut from remaining pastry.

4 Bake in hot oven (425°) 40 minutes, or until pastry is golden.

Raisin Rounds

Bake at 425° for 10 minutes. Makes 2 dozen

    1 egg
    ¾ cup granulated sugar
    1 cup seedless raisins
    1 tablespoon grated orange peel
    ¼ cup orange juice
    ½ cup chopped walnuts
    1 package piecrust mix

1 Beat egg slightly in a small saucepan; stir in sugar, raisins and orange peel and juice.

2 Heat very slowly, stirring constantly, to boiling; simmer 3 to 5 minutes, or until thick; remove from heat. Stir in walnuts; cool.

3 Prepare piecrust mix, following label directions, or make pastry from your favorite double-crust recipe. Roll out, half at a time, ¼ inch thick, on a lightly floured pastry cloth or board. Cut out 48 rounds with a 2-inch scalloped cookie cutter; cut 1-inch circles from half of the rounds.

4 Spread a generous teaspoonful of fruit mixture on each whole round; top each with a pastry ring; press around edges with a fork to seal. Place on large cookie sheets.

5 Bake in hot oven (425°) 10 minutes, or until lightly golden. Remove to wire racks to cool.

CUSTARDS AND CREAM PIES

Basic Custard Pie

Bake at 450° for 10 minutes, then at 300° for about 45 minutes. Makes one 9-inch pie

    1 recipe PLAIN PASTRY I (recipe precedes)
    4 eggs
    ¼ teaspoon salt
    ⅛ teaspoon ground nutmeg
    3 cups milk
    ½ cup sugar
    1 teaspoon vanilla

1 Make PLAIN PASTRY I. Roll out to a 12-inch round on a lightly floured board; fit into a 9-inch pie plate; trim overhang to ½ inch; turn under and flute. Chill while preparing filling.

2 Beat eggs slightly with salt and nutmeg in a medium-size bowl; stir in remaining ingredients.

3 Set pie plate on a cookie sheet; place on rack in oven; strain custard mixture into prepared shell.

4 Bake in hot oven (450°) 10 minutes; reduce heat to slow (300°); bake 45 minutes longer or until center is almost set but still soft. (Do not overbake, as custard will set as it cools). Cool pie completely on wire rack.

Toasted Coconut Custard Pie

Coconut bakes in the velvety-smooth filling and plenty more goes on top.

Bake at 425° for 5 minutes, then at 325° for 50 minutes. Makes one 9-inch pie

1499

PIES THEY'LL APPLAUD

1 recipe PLAIN PASTRY I *(recipe precedes)*
4 eggs
½ cup sugar
  Dash of salt
3 cups milk, scalded
1½ teaspoons vanilla
½ teaspoon grated lemon peel
1 can (3½ ounces) flaked coconut
  Red currant jelly

1 Prepare PLAIN PASTRY I. Roll out to a 12-inch round on a lightly floured pastry cloth or board; fit into a 9-inch pie plate. Trim overhang to ½ inch; turn under, flush with rim; flute to make a stand-up edge. Prick slightly with a fork.

2 Bake in hot oven (425°) 5 minutes, or just until pastry is set but not brown; remove from oven. Lower heat to slow (325°).
3 While pastry bakes, beat eggs slightly in a medium-size bowl; stir in sugar and salt, then scalded milk *very slowly,* and vanilla. Strain into a 4-cup measure or pitcher; stir in lemon peel.
4 Sprinkle ½ cup of the coconut into partly baked pastry shell; set pie plate on oven shelf; pour in custard mixture. Spread remaining coconut in a shallow pan.
5 Bake pie in slow oven (325°) 50 minutes, or until center is almost set but still soft. (Do not overbake, as custard will set as it cools.) Toast coconut in same oven 10 minutes, or just until golden. Cool pie completely on a wire rack.
6 When ready to serve, spoon toasted coconut in 6 or 8 mounds on top of pie; top each with a small spoonful of red currant jelly.

Macaroon Custard Tarts
Bake shells at 425° for 15 minutes. Makes 6 servings

½ package piecrust mix
1 package (3 ounces) egg-custard mix
1⅓ cups milk
1 cup thawed frozen whipped topping
½ cup macaroon crumbs
  Mandarin-orange segments, well drained

1 Prepare piecrust mix, following label directions, or make pastry from your favorite single-crust recipe. Roll out, ⅛ inch thick, on a lightly floured pastry cloth or board. Cut into 4½-inch

Mix-based Macaroon Custard Tarts go together fast.

Basic Custard Pie at the peak of perfection. The crust is crisp and the filling neither too soft nor too stiff.

1500

rounds; fit each into a 3-inch tart-shell pan. Prick shells well all over with a fork. Set pans in a jelly-roll pan for easy handling.

2 Bake in hot oven (425°) 15 minutes, or until golden. Cool completely in pans on a wire rack.

3 Prepare custard mix with the 1⅓ cups milk, following label directions; pour into a medium-size bowl. Set bowl in a pan of ice and water to speed cooling. Chill, stirring several times, until completely cold; fold in whipped topping and macaroon crumbs. Spoon into tart shells.

4 Chill several hours, or until firm. Just before serving, garnish each tart with a rosette of mandarin-orange segments.

Coconut Cream Pie

Under the tart apricot topper is a rich cream filling laced with freshly grated coconut. Recipe tells how to prepare the coconut.
Bake shell at 425° for 15 minutes. Makes one 9-inch pie.

    ½ package piecrust mix
    ⅔ cup sugar
    ¼ cup cornstarch
    3 tablespoons all-purpose flour
    ½ teaspoon salt
    2½ cups milk
    2 eggs
    2 tablespoons butter or margarine
    2 teaspoons vanilla
    ¼ teaspoon lemon extract
    1½ cups cream for whipping
    1 cup grated fresh coconut
      OR: 1 can (about 4 ounces) flaked coconut
    ¾ cup apricot preserves
      Red and yellow food colorings
      ½ cup shredded fresh coconut

1 Prepare piecrust mix, following label directions, or make pastry from your own single-crust recipe.

2 Roll out to a 12-inch round on a lightly floured pastry cloth or board; fit into a 9-inch pie plate. Trim overhang to ½ inch; turn under, flush with rim; flute edge. Prick shell well all over with a fork.

3 Bake in hot oven (425°) 15 minutes, or until golden; cool.

4 Mix sugar, cornstarch, flour and salt in the top of a double boiler; stir in milk. Cook over simmering water, stirring constantly, until mixture thickens; cover. Cook 15 minutes longer; remove from heat.

5 Beat eggs slightly in a small bowl; slowly stir in about half of the hot mixture; stir back into remaining mixture in double boiler. Cook over simmering water, stirring constantly, 3 minutes;

remove from heat. Stir in butter or margarine, 1 teaspoon of the vanilla and lemon extract. Pour into a medium-size bowl; cover surface with wax paper or transparent wrap; chill.

6 Beat ½ cup of the cream until stiff in a small bowl. Fold the 1 cup grated (or 1 cup flaked) coconut into chilled pudding, then fold in whipped cream.

7 Whip ½ cup of the apricot preserves until soft in a small bowl; spread in cooled pastry shell; spoon cream filling on top. Chill at least 2 hours, or until firm enough to cut.

8 Just before serving, combine remaining ¼ cup apricot preserves and 1 teaspoon vanilla in a small bowl; stir in several drops each red and yellow food colorings to tint a deep apricot color. Add remaining 1 cup cream; beat until stiff. Spread on top of pie; garnish with shredded coconut or rest of flaked coconut.

Note—To fix a fresh coconut: Look for the three "eyes" at one end of the coconut and puncture each with an ice pick or punch and hammer; drain milk into a bowl and chill to serve over fruit or stir into curry sauce. Crack shell open in a vise or use a hammer. (Brown shell will fall away easily in big chunks.) Shave thin brown covering from each piece of the coconut meat with a vegetable parer; grate enough meat to measure 1 cup for pie filling and shred ½ cup for garnish. Wrap any remaining; keep chilled.

Chocolate Pouf Pie

Snowy crown and candy curls trim layers of rich chocolate-and-coffee cream.
Bake shell at 375° for 10 minutes. Makes one 9-inch pie

    1⅓ cups crushed vanilla wafers
    ¼ cup sugar
    ½ teaspoon ground cinnamon
    4 tablespoons (½ stick) butter or margarine, softened
    2 packages (about 4 ounces each) vanilla-flavor pudding and pie filling mix
    4½ cups milk
    2 teaspoons instant coffee powder
    1 teaspoon vanilla
    2 bars (about 2 ounces each) plain milk-chocolate candy
    1 package whipped topping mix

1 Mix crushed vanilla wafers, sugar, ¼ teaspoon of the cinnamon and butter or margarine until well blended in a medium-size bowl. Press

1501

into bottom and around edge of a 9-inch pie plate.

2 Bake in moderate oven (375°) 10 minutes, or until crust is set; cool.

3 Combine 1 package of the pudding mix with 2 cups of the milk in a medium-size saucepan; cook, following label directions; remove from heat. Stir in instant coffee powder, remaining ¼ teaspoon cinnamon and ½ teaspoon of the vanilla; cool. Pour into cooled shell; chill.

4 Shave long thin strips from candy bars with a vegetable parer to make 16 curls; set aside for garnish.

5 Prepare remaining package of pudding mix with another 2 cups of the milk, following label directions; remove from heat. Break up remaining candy bars and stir in until completely melted; cool. Spoon over coffee layer. Chill pie until firm.

6 Prepare whipped topping mix with remaining ½ cup milk and ½ teaspoon vanilla, following label directions; drop by spoonfuls around edge of pie; garnish with saved chocolate curls.

●

Triple Fruit Tart

Rosy strawberries, mandarin oranges and tangy pineapple sparkle atop a super-smooth cream layer.

Bake shell at 425° for 15 minutes. Makes one 9-inch pie

½ package piecrust mix
1 package vanilla-flavor whipped-dessert mix
1 cup milk
½ cup cream for whipping
½ pint strawberries
1 can (11 ounces) mandarin-orange segments
1 can (about 14 ounces) pineapple tidbits
½ cup apple jelly

1 Prepare piecrust mix, following label directions, or make pastry from your favorite single-crust recipe.

2 Roll out to a 12-inch round on a lightly floured pastry cloth or board; fit into a 9-inch pie plate. Trim overhang to ½ inch; turn under, flush with rim; flute edge. Prick shell well all over with a fork. (If you wish to make a rope edge on pastry shell, turn overhang under, flush with rim, then pinch to make a stand-up edge. Press a pencil or skewer diagonally into stand-up edge all the way around to make wide, evenly spaced ridges.)

1502

Clockwise from lower left: Coconut Cream Pie, Pinwheel Peach Pie, Chocolate Pouf Pie, Banana Jubilee Pie, Butterscotch Pecan Meringue Pie and, in the center, glistening with fruit, Triple Fruit Tart.

3 Bake in hot oven (425°) 15 minutes, or until golden; cool completely on a wire rack.
4 Prepare whipped-dessert mix with the 1 cup milk, following label directions; chill 1 hour, or until very thick.
5 Beat cream until stiff in a small bowl; beat chilled dessert mix; fold in whipped cream. Spoon into cooled pastry shell; chill.
6 Wash strawberries and hull. Drain syrups from mandarin-orange segments and pineapple and save to add to a fruit beverage.
7 Heat apple jelly slowly until melted in a small saucepan; cool.
8 Arrange the mandarin-orange segments, then pineapple tidbits in circles around edge of filled pie. Place 1 whole strawberry, tip end up, in center; halve remaining; arrange, overlapping, around whole strawberry. Spoon cooled jelly over all to glaze. Chill pie about an hour before cutting.

Pinwheel Peach Pie

Please fruit- and cream-pie fans at the same time with this double-good treat.
Bake shell at 425° for 15 minutes. Makes one 9-inch pie

  ½ *package piecrust mix*
  2 *cups cream for whipping*
  2 *packages vanilla-flavor instant pudding mix*
1½ *cups milk*
1½ *teaspoons vanilla*
  1 *package (10 ounces) frozen sliced peaches, thawed*
  2 *teaspoons cornstarch*
  ½ *teaspoon lemon juice*
  ½ *teaspoon almond extract*

1 Prepare piecrust mix, following label directions, or make pastry from your favorite single-crust recipe.
2 Roll out to a 12-inch round on a lightly floured pastry cloth or board; fit into a 9-inch pie plate. Trim overhang to ½ inch; turn under, flush with rim; flute to make a stand-up edge. Prick shell well all over with a fork.
3 Bake in hot oven (425°) 15 minutes, or until golden; cool completely on a wire rack.
4 Beat cream until stiff in a medium-size bowl. Combine instant pudding mix with milk and vanilla; beat 1 minute; fold in whipped cream until no streaks of white remain.
5 Spoon into cooled pastry shell, leaving a 3-inch well in center. Chill while preparing peaches.

6 Drain syrup from peaches into a cup; place peaches in a small bowl.
7 Stir syrup into cornstarch until smooth in a small saucepan; cook, stirring constantly, until mixture thickens and boils 3 minutes. Stir in lemon juice and almond extract; pour over peaches; cool.
8 Spoon into center well in pie, arranging some of the peach slices in a pretty pattern on top. Chill several hours, or until firm enough to cut. *Note*—If you wish to make a fancy edge on pastry shell, prepare 1 package piecrust mix. Roll out half; fit into pie plate; trim overhang to ¼ inch and press under rim of plate. (This helps to prevent shrinking.) Roll out remaining pastry and cut out about 25 heart shapes with a truffle cutter. Moisten rim of pastry shell with water; lay heart cutouts around edge; press lightly with fingertip to hold in place. Bake any remaining pastry for nibbles.

Peach Twinkles

Glazed plump peach halves sparkle atop a rich cream filling in tart shells.
Bake shells at 425° for 15 minutes. Makes 12 tarts

  1 *recipe* PLAIN PASTRY II *(recipe precedes)*
  1 *package (about 4 ounces) vanilla-flavor instant pudding mix*
  ¾ *cups light cream or table cream*
  ½ *teaspoon rum flavoring or extract*
  2 *cans (1 pound, 14 ounces each) peach halves, well drained*
12 *whole cloves*
  ½ *cup apricot preserves (from a 12-ounce jar)*

1 Prepare pastry, following recipe or use 1 package piecrust mix, following label directions.
2 Roll out, ¼ at a time, ¼ inch thick, on a lightly floured pastry cloth or board; cut each into three 6-inch rounds, using a saucer for pattern. Fit into 3-inch tart-shell pans, pressing firmly against bottoms and sides; trim any overhang. Prick well all over with a fork. Repeat with remaining pastry to make 12 shells.
3 Bake in hot oven (425°) 15 minutes, or until golden; cool completely in pans on wire racks, then remove carefully.
4 Prepare pudding mix with cream and rum flavoring or extract, following label directions. Spoon into cooled tart shells, dividing evenly; chill.
5 Place a drained peach half, rounded side up, on top of filling in each shell. (Save any remaining peach halves for a salad or dessert for another meal.) If you wish to make fluted peaches, mark center of rounded side of each peach half with a wooden pick. Starting here,

Blueberry Cream Pie, a flotilla of blueberries on a sea of cream cheese under an apple-jelly glaze.

make a curved cut about ⅛ inch deep to edge with a sharp thin-blade knife. Repeat around peach, making 8 evenly spaced cuts. Make a second curved cut just behind each line, slanting knife slightly, then lift out the narrow strip of peach. Place peaches on filling as above. Pull out picks; replace each with a whole clove.
6 Heat apricot preserves, stirring constantly, just until melted in a small saucepan. Press through a sieve, then brush over peach halves. Chill.

Strawberry Ice Cream Pie
It's as pretty as the first spring tulip, and just see how quickly it goes together.
Makes one 10-inch pie

 1 package (6 ounces) strawberry-flavor gelatin
2½ cups hot water
 2 pints vanilla ice cream
12 ladyfingers, separated (24 pieces)
 1 cup (about ½ pint) strawberries, washed and hulled

1 Dissolve gelatin in hot water in medium-size bowl. Stir in ice cream, a big spoonful at a time, until melted. Chill 20 minutes, or until mixture mounds slightly on a spoon.
2 While filling chills, arrange ladyfingers, spoke-fashion, around rim of 10-inch pie plate; lay any remaining in bottom.
3 Spoon chilled gelatin mixture into prepared pie plate; chill several hours, or until firm.
4 When ready to serve, quarter strawberries lengthwise, saving 1 large whole one. Arrange slices in two overlapping rings on top of pie; place whole berry in center.
5 Cut into thin wedges; it's rich.

1505

Blueberry Cream Pie
These regal berries, asparkle with a tart glaze, hide a creamy cheese-rich layer.
Bake shell at 425° for 12 minutes. Makes one 9-inch pie

1½ cups sifted all-purpose flour
 ½ teaspoon salt
 ½ cup shortening

3 tablespoons cold water
1 cup blueberries
1½ cups milk
1 package (3 or 4 ounces) cream cheese
1 package vanilla-flavor instant pudding mix
¼ cup apple jelly
1 tablespoon water
2 teaspoons lemon juice

1 Sift flour and salt into a medium-size bowl; cut in shortening with a pastry blender until mixture is crumbly. Sprinkle the 3 tablespoons cold water over, 1 tablespoon at a time; mix lightly with a fork just until pastry holds together and leaves side of bowl clean.
2 Roll out to a 12-inch round on a lightly floured pastry cloth or board; fit into a 9-inch pie plate. Trim overhang to ½ inch; turn under, flush with rim; flute to make a stand-up edge. Prick shell well all over with a fork.
3 If you wish to make the fancy edge as pictured, fit pastry into pie plate; trim overhang to ½ inch; press pastry under edge of rim. (This prevents shrinking.)
4 Cut out about 20 leaf and large and small flower shapes from trimmings with truffle cutters. Moisten rim of pastry shell with water; lay leaf cutouts, about an inch apart, around rim; stack large and small flowers between, as pictured.
5 Bake in hot oven (425°) 12 minutes or until golden; cool completely on a wire rack.
6 While pastry bakes, wash blueberries and stem.
7 Blend milk into cream cheese until smooth in a medium-size bowl; add instant pudding mix and beat slowly 1 minute; pour into cooled pastry shell. Arrange blueberries on top.
8 Combine apple jelly, the 1 tablespoon water and lemon juice in a small saucepan; heat slowly, stirring constantly, just until jelly melts; cool slightly. Spoon over blueberries. Chill until firm.

1506

Lemon Blossom Tart
Bake shell at 400° for 20 minutes. Makes one 9-inch pie

1 package piecrust mix
2 tablespoons sugar (for pastry)
4 eggs
½ cup sugar (for filling)
2 teaspoons grated lemon peel
¼ cup lemon juice
4 tablespoons (½ stick) butter or margarine
1 cup cream for whipping

1 Combine piecrust mix, the 2 tablespoons sugar and 1 of the eggs in a medium-size bowl. Mix with a fork until well blended.
2 Press evenly over bottom and up side of a 9-inch round layer-cake pan, making rim even with edge of pan. (Shell will be thick.) Prick well all over with a fork.
3 Bake in hot oven (400°) 20 minutes, or until golden. Cool completely in pan on a wire rack.
4 Beat remaining 3 eggs slightly in the top of a double boiler; stir in the ½ cup sugar, lemon peel and juice and butter or margarine. Cook, stirring constantly, over hot (not boiling) water 10 minutes, or until very thick. Pour into a medium-size bowl; chill until completely cold.
5 Beat cream until stiff in a medium-size bowl; fold into lemon custard.
6 Remove pastry shell carefully from pan; place on a large serving plate; spoon lemon filling into shell. Garnish with a pinwheel of candied lemon slices, if you wish. Chill 1 to 2 hours before serving.

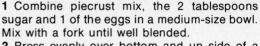

Banana Jubilee Pie
For this dessert winner, dark cherry sauce tops the richest made-from-scratch filling.
Bake shell at 425° for 15 minutes. Makes one 9-inch pie

½ package piecrust mix
¾ cup sugar
⅓ cup sifted all-purpose flour
¼ teaspoon salt
2 cups milk, scalded
3 eggs
2 tablespoons butter or margarine
1 teaspoon vanilla
3 medium-size firm ripe bananas
JUBILEE SAUCE (recipe follows)

1 Prepare piecrust mix, following label directions, or make pastry from your favorite single-crust recipe.
2 Roll out to a 12-inch round on a lightly floured pastry cloth or board; fit into a 9-inch pie plate. Trim overhang to ½ inch; turn under, flush with rim; flute to make a stand-up edge. Prick shell well all over with a fork.
3 Bake in hot oven (425°) 15 minutes, or until golden; cool completely on a wire rack.
4 Mix sugar, flour and salt in a medium-size heavy saucepan; slowly stir in scalded milk. Cook, stirring constantly, over medium heat until mixture thickens and boils 1 minute; remove from heat.

5 Beat eggs in a small bowl; slowly stir in a generous ½ cup of the hot mixture; stir back into remaining mixture in pan. Cook, stirring constantly, over medium heat 3 minutes, or until mixture thickens again and mounds softly; remove from heat. Stir in butter or margarine and vanilla; cool.

6 Peel 1 of the bananas and slice; place in a layer in cooled pastry shell; pour in half of the filling. Repeat with another banana and remaining filling. Chill 4 to 5 hours, or until set.

7 Just before serving, peel remaining banana and slice diagonally; arrange slices in a rosette in center of pie. Top with one or two spoonfuls of the JUBILEE SAUCE; serve remaining sauce separately.

Note—If you wish to make a fancy edge on pastry shell, prepare 1 package piecrust mix. Roll out half; fit into pie plate; trim overhang flush with rim. Roll out remaining pastry to a strip, 18x2; trim edges even, then cut lengthwise into four ½-inch-wide strips. Moisten rim of pastry shell with water; twist each two strips of pastry together and place around rim; press lightly with fingertip to hold in place. Bake any remaining pastry for nibbles.

Jubilee Sauce
Easy to put together, it gives an old favorite a new flavor and look.
Makes about 2 cups

1 can (1 pound) pitted dark sweet cherries
Water
2 tablespoons sugar
1 tablespoon cornstarch
2 teaspoons rum flavoring or extract

1 Drain syrup from cherries into a 1-cup measure; add water to make 1 cup.
2 Mix sugar and cornstarch in a small saucepan; stir in cherry liquid. Cook, stirring constantly, until sauce thickens and boils 3 minutes; stir in rum flavoring or extract and cherries. Cool.

Praline Pumpkin Pie
A soft, candylike, nut-studded layer hides beneath its creamy golden custard.
Bake at 450° for 10 minutes, then at 350° for 50 minutes. Makes one 9-inch pie

Praline Layer
1 stick piecrust mix
3 tablespoons butter or margarine
⅓ cup firmly packed brown sugar
⅓ cup chopped pecans

Custard Layer
1 cup evaporated milk
½ cup water
3 eggs
1½ cups canned pumpkin
½ cup granulated sugar
½ cup firmly packed brown sugar
1½ teaspoons pumpkin-pie spice
1 teaspoon salt
½ cup cream, whipped
PRALINE LACE CONES (recipe follows)

1 Make praline layer: Prepare piecrust mix, following label directions, or make single-crust pastry from your own favorite recipe. Roll out to a 12-inch round on lightly floured pastry cloth or board; fit into a 9-inch pie plate; trim overhang; turn under and flute.
2 Cream butter or margarine with brown sugar in small bowl; stir in pecans. Press over bottom of prepared shell in an even layer.
3 Bake in very hot oven (450°) 10 minutes; remove; cool on wire rack 10 minutes. Reduce heat to moderate (350°).
4 Make custard layer: Scald evaporated milk with water in small saucepan. Beat eggs slightly in large bowl; stir in pumpkin, granulated sugar, ½ cup brown sugar, pumpkin-pie spice and salt; beat in scalded milk mixture. Pour into cooled pastry shell.
5 Bake in moderate oven (350°) 50 minutes, or until center is set but still soft. (Do not overbake, as custard will set as it cools.) Cool completely on wire rack.
6 Top with a crown of whipped cream; decorate with PRALINE LACE CONES.

Praline Lace Cones
They're shattery bits of goodness to crown your pie. Perfect for tea parties, too.
Bake at 300° for 10 minutes. Makes about 3 dozen

4 tablespoons (½ stick) butter or margarine
½ cup firmly packed brown sugar
1 egg
¼ cup finely chopped pecans
2 tablespoons all-purpose flour
¼ teaspoon salt

1 Cream butter or margarine with sugar until fluffy-light in bowl. Beat in egg; stir in pecans, flour and salt.

1507

2 Drop batter by half-teaspoonfuls, about 5 inches apart, on lightly greased cookie sheet; spread each into a very thin 2½-inch round. (Make only 2 cookies at a time for easier handling. To save time, use two cookie sheets; bake one batch while shaping the other.)

3 Bake in slow oven (300°) 10 minutes, until golden-brown. Cool on cookie sheet 1 minute, or just until firm enough to hold their shape.

4 Cut in half with a sharp knife, then loosen with spatula. Quickly roll each half into a tiny cone shape; place on wire rack to cool and crisp. (If cookies become too brittle to shape easily, return cookie sheet to oven for 30 seconds to soften.)

Note—Bake and shape 16 cones for pie. If you wish, bake the rest as thin flat cookies without halving.

Pumpkin-Apple Pie-ettes

Applesauce blends with mellow pumpkin in these mildly spiced little pies.

Bake at 400° for 40 minutes. Makes 6 tarts

1 package piecrust mix
  OR: 1 recipe PLAIN PASTRY II *(recipe precedes)*
1 cup evaporated milk
½ cup water
3 eggs
½ cup granulated sugar
½ cup firmly packed brown sugar
1 teaspoon salt
½ teaspoon ground cinnamon
½ teaspoon ground mace
1 cup pumpkin (from a 1-pound can)
1 cup canned applesauce
½ cup cream for whipping
1 small red-skin apple, quartered, cored and sliced thin

1 Prepare piecrust mix, following label directions, or mix up PLAIN PASTRY II.

2 Roll out, ⅓ at a time, ⅛ inch thick, on a lightly floured pastry cloth or board; cut each into two 6-inch rounds, using a saucer for pattern.

3 Fit each into a ¾-cup-size tart pan, pressing firmly against bottom and side. Trim overhang to ½ inch, turn under, flush with rim; flute.

4 Scald evaporated milk with water in a small saucepan. Beat eggs slightly in a medium-size bowl; stir in granulated and brown sugars, salt, cinnamon and mace. Stir in hot milk mixture slowly; blend in pumpkin and applesauce. Pour into prepared tart shells, dividing evenly.

5 Bake in hot oven (400°) 40 minutes, or until centers are set but still soft. (Do not overbake, as custard will set as it cools.) Cool completely on wire rack.

6 Just before serving, loosen tarts around edges with tip of knife, then tip pans, sliding tarts onto individual serving plates.

7 Beat cream until stiff in a small bowl; spoon in puffs on tarts; garnish with a few thin slices of apple. Tarts are best served the day they are made, as filling tends to pull away from crust if chilled overnight.

New-Fashioned Low-Calorie Pumpkin Pie

Bake at 350° for 1 hour. Makes 8 servings, 121 calories each
Conventional recipe, 240 calories per serving.

  SKINNY PIECRUST *(recipe precedes)*
1 cup canned pumpkin
2 eggs
1¼ cups skim milk
½ tablespoon cornstarch
¼ cup firmly packed brown sugar
  Sugar substitute to equal ¼ cup sugar
¼ teaspoon salt
½ teaspoon ground cinnamon
⅛ teaspoon ground allspice
⅛ teaspoon ground ginger
⅛ teaspoon ground nutmeg

1 Prepare pastry. Roll out to an 11-inch round on a lightly floured board. Fit into an 8-inch pie plate; turn edge under; flute.

2 Put all remaining ingredients in your blender

Pastry leaves handsomely trim a classic pumpkin pie.

Underneath a whipped cream cloud, studded with crispy Praline Lace Cones is a rich pumpkin pie. Put them together and you've created cool Praline Pumpkin Pie.

or in electric-mixer bowl and beat on high speed until smooth.

3 Pour into prepared piecrust; bake in a moderate oven (350°) for 60 minutes, until crust is lightly browned and filling is set.

4 Roll out pastry trimmings; cut into leaves or other fancy shapes with cookie cutter; place on cookie sheet. Bake cutouts with pie, or after pie is out of oven and you have room, just until golden. Arrange on top of pie.

●

Harvest Yam Pie

Bake shell at 350° for 8 minutes. Makes one 9-inch pie

> 1 cup fine zwieback crumbs (16 pieces)
> ½ cup crunchy nutlike cereal nuggets
> ¼ cup firmly packed light brown sugar

> 6 tablespoons (¾ stick) butter or margarine, melted
> 1 can (1 pound) yams or sweet potatoes, drained
> 1 package (3 ounces) egg-custard mix
> 1½ cups milk
> ¼ cup maple-blended syrup
> 1 teaspoon pumpkin-pie spice
> 1 container (4½ ounces) frozen whipped topping, thawed

1 Blend zwieback crumbs, cereal, brown sugar and melted butter or margarine in a large bowl. Press evenly over bottom and side of a 9-inch pie plate.

2 Bake in moderate oven (350°) 8 minutes, or until set. Cool completely in pie plate on a wire rack.

3 Mash yams well with a fork in a large saucepan; stir in custard mix, milk, syrup and pumpkin-pie spice. Heat over medium heat, stirring constantly, to boiling; press through a sieve into a large bowl. Cool, stirring often, 30 minutes. Fold in half of the whipped topping; spoon into cooled pie shell. Chill several hours, or until firm. Just before serving, spoon remaining topping in a ring on pie.

●

Fruited Sour Cream Pie
Bake at 400° for 40 minutes. Makes one 9-inch pie

½ package piecrust mix
3 eggs
1 cup sugar
¼ teaspoon salt
¼ teaspoon ground cinnamon
1½ cups dairy sour cream
1 package (8 ounces) pitted dates, cut up
½ cup golden raisins

1 Prepare piecrust mix, following label directions, or make pastry from your favorite single-crust recipe. Roll out to a 12-inch round on a lightly floured pastry cloth or board; fit into a 9-inch pie plate. Trim overhang to ½ inch; turn under, flush with rim; flute to make a stand-up edge.
2 Beat eggs until foamy in a medium-size bowl. Stir in sugar, salt, cinnamon and sour cream, until blended. Stir in dates and raisins. Pour into prepared pastry shell, spreading evenly.
3 Bake in hot oven (400°) 40 minutes, or until filling is puffy and set. Cool completely on a wire rack. Serve plain or with scoops of ice cream, if you wish.
Note—This is a rich pie and can be cut into 8 to 12 wedges.

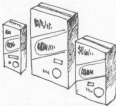

1510

Harvest Pecan Pie
Bake at 425° for 10 minutes, then at 350° for 30 minutes. Makes one 9-inch pie

½ package piecrust mix
2 cups pecans
½ cup (1 stick) butter or margarine
1 cup sugar
4 eggs
½ cup dairy sour cream
2 teaspoons grated lemon peel
1 cup chopped pitted dates
1 cup seedless raisins

1 Prepare piecrust mix, following label directions, or make pastry from your favorite single-crust recipe. Roll out to a 12-inch round on a lightly floured pastry cloth or board; fit into a 9-inch pie plate. Trim overhang to ½ inch; turn under, flush with rim; flute to make a stand-up edge.
2 Set aside ½ cup of the pecans for topping, then chop remainder coarsely.
3 Cream butter or margarine with sugar until fluffy in a large bowl; beat in eggs, 1 at a time, until well blended. Stir in sour cream, lemon peel, the chopped pecans, dates and raisins. Spoon into prepared pastry shell; arrange remaining pecans over filling.
4 Bake in hot oven (425°) 10 minutes. Lower oven temperature to moderate (350°); continue baking 30 minutes, or until filling is set. Cool pie completely on a wire rack.

Sour Cream Pecan Pie
It's a spicy old-time favorite, rich with nuts and fruit. Pecan halves perch atop pastry cutouts for its fancy topper.
Bake at 425° for 10 minutes, then at 325° for 30 minutes. Makes one 9-inch pie

1 stick piecrust mix
OR: 1 recipe PLAIN PASTRY I (recipe precedes)
Pecan halves
3 whole eggs
1 egg, separated
1 cup sugar (for filling)
1 tablespoon all-purpose flour
¼ teaspoon ground cardamom
1 cup dairy sour cream
1 cup chopped pecans
½ cup finely chopped dried apricots
Sugar

1 Prepare piecrust mix, following label directions, or make PLAIN PASTRY I. Roll out to a 12-inch round on lightly floured pastry cloth or board; fit into a 9-inch pie plate. Trim overhang to ½ inch; turn under, flush with rim. Flute to make a stand-up edge, or form a ropelike edge by pressing a pencil diagonally around stand-up rim to make ridges.
2 Roll out pastry trimmings ⅛ inch thick; cut into tiny rounds with a 1-inch cutter. Place on cookie sheet; top each with a pecan half, pressing down to hold in place. Set aside for Step 4.

3 Beat whole eggs and egg white until light in large bowl. (Save remaining egg yolk for next step.) Gradually beat in 1 cup sugar until well blended; stir in flour and cardamom. Fold in sour cream, chopped pecans and apricots. Pour into prepared pastry shell.

4 Beat saved egg yolk in cup; brush over pecan-topped pastries; sprinkle with sugar.

5 Bake pie and cutouts in hot oven (425°) 10 minutes; remove cutouts and cool on wire rack. Reduce heat to slow (325°). Bake pie 30 minutes longer, or until center is firm and pastry is golden. Cool on wire rack; arrange pastry trims, centering one and placing remaining in a ring, on top.

MERINGUE PIES

Lemon Meringue Pie

Smooth, fresh-lemon flavor; dreamy, cloudlike topping, and a neat serving every time—no wonder that this is the best lemon pie ever.
Bake the shell in a 450° oven for 8 to 10 minutes. Bake the meringue puffs at 425° for 3 to 5 minutes. Makes one 8-inch pie

½ package piecrust mix
1⅓ cups sugar (for filling)
½ cup cornstarch
¼ teaspoon salt

The great American classic: billowy Lemon Meringue Pie. The filling should be good and tart, the crust flaky.

1¾ cups water
4 eggs, separated
2 tablespoons butter or margarine
1 tablespoon grated lemon peel
½ cup lemon juice (about 4 lemons)
¼ teaspoon cream of tartar
½ cup sugar (for meringue)

1 Prepare piecrust mix, following label directions, or make pastry from your favorite single-crust recipe. Roll out to a 10-inch round on a lightly floured pastry board; fit into an 8-inch pie plate. Trim overhang to ½ inch; turn under, flush with rim; scallop the edge with an inverted teaspoon, pressing down hard for each cut to form design.
2 Bake in hot oven (450°) 8 to 10 minutes, or until golden brown; cool.
3 Combine 1⅓ cups sugar, cornstarch and salt in a medium-size saucepan; gradually stir in water.
4 Cook over medium heat, stirring constantly, until mixture comes to boiling and is thickened. Boil 1 minute. Remove from heat.
5 Beat egg yolks slightly in a small bowl; slowly blend in about ½ cup of the hot cornstarch mixture; slowly stir back into remaining mixture in saucepan. Cook, stirring constantly, over low heat 2 minutes; remove from heat. (Do not overcook.) Stir in butter or margarine, lemon peel and lemon juice; pour into cooled pastry shell. Cover with transparent wrap; refrigerate until cold, about 3 hours.
6 Beat egg whites with cream of tartar until foamy-white and double in volume in a medium-size bowl; sprinkle in remaining ½ cup sugar, 1 tablespoon at a time, beating all the time until sugar dissolves completely and meringue stands in firm peaks.
7 Using a pastry bag with a large notched tip, press meringue into 10 to 12 large puffs on a greased and lightly floured cookie sheet. If you do not have a pastry bag, you can spoon the meringue into puffs.
8 Bake in hot oven (425°) 3 to 5 minutes, or just until peaks turn golden. Cool on cookie sheet. When the puffs are cool, carefully place on the cold pie with a small spatula. Garnish with lemon slices, if you wish.

Lemon Meringue Puff Pie
Bake pie shell at 425° 15 minutes, meringue at 350° for 12 minutes. Makes one 9-inch pie

½ package piecrust mix or 1 recipe PLAIN PASTRY I (recipe precedes)
1¾ cups sugar (for filling)
4 tablespoons cornstarch
4 tablespoons all-purpose flour

¼ teaspoon salt
2 cups water
4 eggs
1 teaspoon grated lemon peel
½ cup lemon juice (about 4 lemons)
2 tablespoons butter or margarine
¼ teaspoon lemon extract
½ cup sugar (for meringue)

1 Prepare pastry following label directions or make PLAIN PASTRY I. Roll out to a 12-inch round on lightly floured pastry cloth or board; fit into a 9-inch pie plate. Trim overhang to ½ inch; turn under, flush with rim. Flute to make a stand-up edge. Prick shell well all over with a fork.
2 Bake in hot oven (425°) 15 minutes, or until golden; cool completely on a wire rack.
3 Combine 1¾ cups sugar, cornstarch, flour and salt in medium-size bowl; stir to mix well.
4 Heat water to boiling in medium-size saucepan. Lower heat to medium; gradually add sugar mixture, stirring constantly with wire whisk or spoon. Cook, stirring constantly, 5 to 7 minutes, or until mixture holds a line when cut with spoon; remove from heat at once. (Do not let mixture boil.)
5 Separate eggs, putting whites in medium-size bowl, yolks in small bowl. Beat egg yolks slightly with a fork; stir in a generous ½ cup of hot mixture; quickly stir back into mixture in saucepan. Cook, stirring constantly, over medium heat 3 minutes, or until mixture thickens again and mounds softly; remove from heat.
6 Stir in lemon peel and juice, and butter or margarine until completely blended; pour into pastry shell.
7 Beat egg whites with lemon extract until foamy-white and double in volume; beat in ½ cup sugar, 1 tablespoon at a time, until meringue forms soft peaks.
8 Pile meringue on filling, spreading to edge of crust. (This keeps meringue from shrinking.)
9 Bake in moderate oven (350°) 12 minutes, or until peaks of meringue are golden-brown. Cool 4 to 5 hours before cutting.
Note—To make the meringue crown on the pie, use just 2 egg whites. Beat with ⅛ teaspoon lemon extract until foamy-white and double in volume in medium-size bowl, then beat in ¼ cup sugar, 1 tablespoon at a time, until meringue forms soft peaks. Drop by teaspoons onto filling to form a crown, then bake as above. Use remaining 2 egg whites to make a meringue topping for another dessert.

For Lemon Meringue Puff Pie, the meringue is piped on with a pastry tube or simply dropped on by spoonsful.

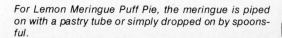

Coconut Meringue Pie
Bake meringue at 350° for 12 minutes. Makes one 9-inch pie

¾ cup sugar
4 tablespoons cornstarch
  Dash of salt
2 cups milk
4 eggs, separated
1 tablespoon butter or margarine
1 teaspoon vanilla
½ cup flaked coconut
1 baked 9-inch pastry shell

1 Mix ½ cup of the sugar, cornstarch and salt in a heavy medium-size saucepan; stir in milk.
2 Cook over low heat, stirring gently but constantly, until mixture thickens and boils 3 minutes.
3 Beat egg yolks well in a small bowl; slowly stir in ½ cup of the hot mixture, then stir back into saucepan. Cook, stirring constantly, 1 minute; remove from heat. Stir in butter or margarine, vanilla and ¼ cup of the coconut. Pour into pastry shell.
4 Beat egg whites until foamy-white in a medium-size bowl; beat in remaining ¼ cup sugar, 1 tablespoon at a time, until meringue stands in firm peaks. Pile onto filling, sealing to edge and swirling into peaks; sprinkle with the remaining ¼ cup flaked coconut.
5 Bake in moderate oven (350°) 12 minutes, or until coconut is toasted and meringue is tipped with brown. (Watch carefully so coconut doesn't burn.) Cool pie at least 5 hours on a wire rack before cutting.

Brown Sugar Meringue Pie
Filling is smooth and satiny, its flavor butterscotchy and rich—so count on 8 wedges from one pie.
Bake shell at 425° for 15 minutes, meringue at 350° for 12 minutes. Makes one 9-inch pie

1 stick piecrust mix
  OR: 1 recipe PLAIN PASTRY I (recipe precedes)
6 tablespoons (¾ stick) butter or margarine
1¼ cups firmly packed dark brown sugar
2 cups scalded milk
1 cup cold milk
½ cup sifted all-purpose flour
½ teaspoon salt
2 eggs, separated
1 teaspoon lemon juice

1514

½ teaspoon vanilla
¼ cup granulated sugar

1 Prepare piecrust mix, following label directions, or make PLAIN PASTRY I. Roll out to a 12-inch round on lightly floured pastry cloth or board; fit into a 9-inch pie plate. Trim overhang to ½ inch; turn under, flush with rim; flute to make a stand-up edge. Prick shell well all over with a fork.
2 Bake in hot oven (425°) 15 minutes, or until golden. Cool completely on wire rack.
3 Combine butter or margarine and brown sugar in medium-size saucepan; heat slowly, stirring constantly, until bubbly. Blend in scalded milk; remove from heat.
4 Stir cold milk into flour and salt in 2-cup measure, then beat until smooth. Gradually stir into hot-milk mixture. Cook over low heat, stirring constantly, 15 minutes, or until mixture thickens; remove from heat.
5 Beat egg yolks slightly with a fork in medium-size bowl. Stir in about a half cupful of hot mixture; quickly stir back into mixture in saucepan. Cook, stirring constantly, 3 minutes, or until mixture mounds lightly on a spoon.
6 Strain into egg-yolk bowl (no need to wash); stir in lemon juice and vanilla. Cool slightly; spoon into shell.
7 Beat egg whites until foamy-white and double in volume in medium-size bowl. Beat in sugar, 1 tablespoon at a time, until meringue forms soft peaks.
8 Drop by teaspoonfuls into mounds to form a crown in center of pie.
9 Bake in moderate oven (350°) 12 minutes, or until meringue is golden. Pie cuts best if allowed to cool for 4 to 5 hours.

Butterscotch Pecan Meringue Pie
Rich-as-candy filling peeks through ribbons of toasty meringue for this sweet show-off.
Bake shell at 400° for 12 minutes. Makes one 9-inch pie

1¾ cups sifted all-purpose flour
1½ teaspoons salt
¼ cup ground pecans
½ cup shortening
1 to 2 tablespoons cold water (for pastry)
6 tablespoons (¾ stick) butter or margarine
1 cup firmly packed dark brown sugar
1 cup water (for filling)
1⅔ cups milk
2 eggs, separated
1 teaspoon vanilla
¼ cup granulated sugar

1 Sift 1¼ cups of the flour and 1 teaspoon of

Another luscious lemon pie, crisp of crust, tart of filling and sky-high with meringue. To give the meringue an unusual trim like this one, spiral slivers of fresh or toasted coconut around the meringue before browning.

the salt into a large bowl; stir in pecans. Cut in shortening with a pastry blender until mixture is crumbly. Sprinkle with the 1 to 2 tablespoons cold water; mix lightly with a fork until pastry holds together and leaves side of bowl clean.

2 Roll out to a 12-inch round on a lightly floured pastry cloth or board; fit into a 9-inch pie plate. Trim overhang to ½ inch; turn under, flush with rim; flute to make a stand-up edge. Prick shell well all over with a fork.

3 Bake in hot oven (400°) 12 minutes, or until golden; cool completely on a wire rack.

4 Melt butter or margarine in a heavy medium-size frying pan; stir in brown sugar and the 1 cup water; heat, stirring constantly, until sugar dissolves; remove from heat.

5 Stir milk into remaining ½ cup flour and ½ teaspoon salt until smooth in a medium-size saucepan; slowly stir in brown-sugar mixture.

6 Cook over low heat, stirring constantly, until mixture thickens and boils 1 minute; remove from heat.

7 Beat egg yolks slightly in a medium-size bowl; slowly stir in a generous ½ cup of the hot mixture; stir back into remaining mixture in pan. Continue cooking, stirring constantly, just until bubbly; remove from heat.

8 Stir in vanilla; cool slightly; pour into cooled pastry shell.

9 Beat egg whites until foamy-white and double in volume in a small bowl; beat in granulated sugar, 1 tablespoon at a time, until meringue forms soft peaks. Drop by teaspoonfuls onto filling to form a lattice top.

10 Bake in moderate oven (350°) 12 minutes, or until meringue is tipped with gold. Cool pie 3 to 4 hours before cutting. Garnish with pecan halves, if you wish.

1516

Another American favorite: Coconut Meringue Pie.

CHIFFON PIES

Rio Lemon Chiffon Pie
Rivulets of melted semisweet chocolate ripple all through the billowiest cream filling.
Bake shell at 425° for 15 minutes. Makes one 9-inch pie

1 recipe PLAIN PASTRY I (recipe precedes)
1 envelope unflavored gelatin
1 cup sugar
¼ cup water
4 eggs, separated
½ teaspoon salt
½ cup lemon juice
1 teaspoon grated lemon peel
1 square semisweet chocolate

1 teaspoon vegetable shortening
1 cup cream for whipping

1 Prepare PLAIN PASTRY I, following recipe, or use ½ package piecrust mix, following label directions. Roll out to a 12-inch round on a lightly floured pastry cloth or board; fit into a 9-inch pie plate. Trim overhang to ½ inch; turn under, flush with rim; flute to make a stand-up edge. Prick well all over with a fork.
2 Bake in hot oven (425°) 15 minutes, or until golden; cool completely on a wire rack.
3 Soften gelatin with ½ cup of the sugar in water in the top of a double boiler. (Set remaining ½ cup sugar aside for Step 8.)
4 Beat egg yolks slightly in a small bowl; stir into gelatin mixture with salt and lemon juice.
5 Cook, stirring constantly, over simmering water 5 minutes, or until mixture thickens

Rio Lemon Chiffon Pie, a South American version of a North American classic, teams chocolate and lemon.

slightly and coats a metal spoon. Strain into a large bowl; stir in lemon peel.

6 Set bowl in a deep pan partly filled with ice and water to speed setting. Chill, stirring often, 5 minutes, or just until as thick as unbeaten egg white.

7 While gelatin mixture chills, melt semisweet chocolate with vegetable shortening in a cup over simmering water.

8 Beat egg whites until foamy-white and double in volume in a medium-size bowl; sprinkle in remaining ½ cup sugar, a tablespoon at a time, beating all the time until sugar completely dissolves and meringue stands in firm peaks. Beat cream until stiff in a second bowl.

9 Fold meringue, then whipped cream into thickened gelatin mixture until no streaks of white remain. Remove from pan of ice and water.

10 Spoon about one third of the gelatin mixture into cooled pastry shell; drizzle with part of the chocolate mixture. Repeat with remaining gelatin mixture and chocolate to make two more layers of each. Chill pie several hours, or until firm.

Lemon Fluff Pie
Start with pie filling mix, then fold in meringue for a light chiffonlike pie.
Bake at 450° for 15 minutes. Makes one 9-inch pie

1 stick piecrust mix
1 package lemon-flavor pie filling mix
  Sugar
  Water
2 eggs, separated
1 tablespoon butter or margarine
2 tablespoons lemon juice
¼ cup sugar (for meringue)
½ cup cream, whipped
½ teaspoon grated lemon peel
2 tablespoons sugar (for topping)

1518

1 Prepare piecrust mix, following label directions, or make pastry from your own favorite recipe; roll out and fit into 9-inch pie plate; flute edge; prick all over with a fork.

2 Bake in very hot oven (450°) 15 minutes, or until golden; cool.

3 Combine pie-filling mix, sugar and water called for in recipe on package for pie filling in medium-size saucepan; beat in egg yolks. (Save egg whites for Step 4.) Cook, following label directions; remove from heat; stir in butter or margarine and lemon juice; cool.

4 Beat egg whites until foamy in medium-size bowl; beat in ½ cup sugar, a tablespoon at a time, until meringue stands in stiff peaks; fold into lemon mixture. Spoon into prepared shell, making deep swirls on top with tip of spoon; chill.

5 Decorate with a crown of whipped cream. Mix lemon peel and 2 tablespoons sugar in small cup; sprinkle over whipped cream.

Lime Sponge Pie
Bake at 425° for 10 minutes, then at 350° for 25 minutes. Makes one 9-inch pie

½ package piecrust mix
3 tablespoons all-purpose flour
¾ cup sugar
¼ teaspoon salt
1½ cups buttermilk
1 teaspoon grated lime peel
¼ cup lime juice
2 tablespoons butter or margarine, melted and cooled
4 drops green food coloring
3 eggs, separated

1 Prepare piecrust mix, following label directions, or make pastry from your favorite single-crust recipe. Roll out to a 12-inch round on a lightly floured pastry cloth or board; fit into a 9-inch pie plate. Trim overhang to ½ inch; turn under, flush with rim; flute to make a stand-up edge.

2 Combine flour, ½ cup of the sugar and salt in a large bowl; mix well; stir in buttermilk, lime peel and juice, butter or margarine and food coloring; beat in egg yolks, one at a time, until mixture is well blended.

3 Beat egg whites until foamy-white and double in volume in a medium-size bowl; beat in remaining ¼ cup sugar, 1 tablespoon at a time, beating all the time until meringue stands in firm peaks. Fold meringue into buttermilk mixture until no streaks of white remain. Spoon into prepared pastry shell.

4 Bake in hot oven (425°) 10 minutes, then lower oven temperature to moderate (350°) and bake 25 minutes longer, or until a knife inserted 1 inch from edge comes out clean. Cool completely on a wire rack.

Cranberry Cream Pie
Bake shell at 425° for 15 minutes. Makes one 9-inch pie

½ package piecrust mix
⅔ cup flaked coconut
1 package (3¼ ounces) vanilla pudding and pie filling mix
2 cups milk
1 egg, separated
1 tablespoon sugar
1 can (8 ounces) whole-berry cranberry sauce
1¾ cups water
1 package (3 ounces) orange-flavor gelatin
1 cup thawed frozen whipped topping

1 Prepare piecrust mix, following label directions, or make pastry from your favorite single-crust recipe. Roll out to a 12-inch round on a lightly floured pastry cloth or board; fit into a 9-inch pie plate. Trim overhang to ½ inch; turn edge under, flush with rim; flute to make a stand-up edge. Prick shell well all over with a fork.
2 Bake in hot oven (425°) 15 minutes, or until golden; cool completely in pie plate on a wire rack.
3 While pastry shell bakes, spread 3 tablespoons of the coconut in a shallow pan; toast in same oven 2 to 3 minutes, watching carefully; cool. Set aside for garnish.
4 Combine pudding mix and milk in a medium-size saucepan; beat in egg yolk. Cook, following label directions; cool slightly. Beat egg white until foamy in a small bowl; beat in sugar until meringue stands in firm peaks. Fold into cooled pudding with remaining coconut. Pour into cooled pastry shell. Chill several hours, or until firm.
5 Combine cranberry sauce and water in a medium-size saucepan; heat, stirring constantly, to boiling; stir in gelatin until dissolved. Chill, stirring several times, until as thick as unbeaten egg white; spoon over cream layer in shell. Chill several hours, or until firm.
6 Just before serving, spoon whipped topping in a ring around edge on pie; sprinkle with toasted coconut.

Sure-fire way to beat the heat: Raspberry Snow Pie.

Raspberry Snow Pie
So rich and creamy—and the kind that coaxes you into having just one more bite.
Bake shell at 425° for 12 minutes. Makes one 9-inch pie

½ package piecrust mix
2 eggs, separated
½ cup sugar
⅛ teaspoon salt
1¼ cups milk
1 envelope unflavored gelatin
1 tablespoon lemon juice
½ teaspoon vanilla
1 cup cream for whipping
2 cups (1 pint) fresh red raspberries, washed and dried

1 Prepare piecrust mix, following label directions, or make pastry from your favorite single-crust recipe. Roll out to a 12-inch round on a lightly floured pastry cloth or board; fit into a 9-inch pie plate. Trim overhang to ½ inch; turn under, flush with rim; flute to make a stand-up edge. Prick shell well all over with a fork.

2 Bake in hot oven (425°) 12 minutes, or until golden; cool completely on a wire rack.

3 Beat egg yolks slightly in the top of a double boiler; stir in ¼ cup of the sugar, salt, and milk; sprinkle gelatin over top to soften.

4 Cook gelatin mixture, stirring constantly, over simmering water 15 minutes, or until gelatin dissolves completely and mixture thickens slightly and coats a metal spoon.

5 Strain into a large bowl; stir in lemon juice and vanilla. Set bowl in a pan of ice and water to speed setting. Chill, stirring often, at room temperature just until as thick as unbeaten egg white.

6 While gelatin mixture chills, beat egg whites until foamy-white and double in volume in a small bowl; sprinkle in remaining ¼ cup sugar, 1 tablespoon at a time, beating all the time until sugar dissolves and meringue stands in firm peaks. Beat cream until stiff in a bowl.

7 Fold meringue, then whipped cream into thickened gelatin mixture; gently fold in raspberries.

8 Spoon into cooled pastry shell. Chill several hours, or until firm.

Strawberry Cream Pie
Bake shell at 450° for 12 minutes. Makes one 9-inch pie

1 frozen ready-to-bake 9-inch piecrust
⅔ cup sugar
4 tablespoons cornstarch
3 tablespoons all-purpose flour
½ teaspoon salt
2 eggs
2½ cups milk
2 tablespoons butter or margarine
1 teaspoon vanilla
½ teaspoon orange extract
2 cups (1 pint) strawberries
½ cup cream for whipping

1 Thaw piecrust, following label directions; place in a 9-inch pie plate; reflute edge to make

Inside the velvety orange-flavored filling of Strawberry Cream Pie are more fresh, sliced strawberries.

1520

Orange Petal Pumpkin Pie is a fluffy, chiffon version of the old-fashioned pumpkin pie everyone loves.

slightly higher. Prick shell well all over with a fork.

2 Bake in very hot oven (450°) 12 minutes, or until golden; cool completely in pie plate on a wire rack.

3 Mix sugar, cornstarch, flour and salt in the top of a double boiler; stir in milk. Cook, stirring often, over simmering water until mixture thickens; cover. Cook 15 minutes longer, or until mixture mounds softly on spoon; remove from heat.

4 Beat eggs slightly in a small bowl; slowly blend in about ½ cup of the hot cornstarch mixture; slowly stir back into remaining mixture in double boiler. Cook, stirring constantly, over simmering water 3 minutes; remove from heat. Stir in butter or margarine until melted, then vanilla and orange extract. Pour into a medium-size bowl; cover. Cool completely.

5 Wash strawberries; reserve half for topping. Hull remainder and halve.

6 Beat cream until stiff in a small bowl; fold into cooled cornstarch mixture. Pour half into prepared pastry shell; place halved strawberries in a single layer on top; spoon in remaining filling. Chill at least 3 hours, or until firm enough to cut.

7 Just before serving, halve reserved berries; arrange, cut side down, on pie.

Orange Petal Pumpkin Pie
Filling is a spicy cloud-light chiffon crowned with puffs of cream and sunny orange sections. Bake at 425° for 15 minutes. Makes one 9-inch pie

    ½ package piecrust mix
    ⅔ cup firmly packed brown sugar
    1 envelope unflavored gelatin
 1¼ teaspoons pumpkin-pie spice
    ¼ teaspoon salt
    4 eggs, separated
    1 cup pumpkin (from a 1-pound can)
    ⅔ cup milk
    ¼ cup granulated sugar
    1 cup cream for whipping
    1 medium-size seedless orange, pared, sectioned and drained

1 Prepare piecrust mix, following label directions, or make pastry from your own favorite one-crust recipe. Roll out to a 12-inch round on a lightly floured pastry cloth or board; fit into a 9-inch pie plate. Trim overhang to ½ inch; turn under, flush with rim; flute to make a stand-up edge. Prick shell well all over with a fork.

2 Bake in hot oven (425°) 15 minutes, or until golden; cool completely on a wire rack.

1521

3 Mix brown sugar, gelatin, pumpkin-pie spice and salt in the top of a large double boiler; beat in egg yolks, pumpkin and milk.

4 Cook, stirring constantly, over simmering water, 15 minutes, or until gelatin dissolves and mixture thickens slightly.

5 Empty bottom of double boiler and fill with ice and water; place top over bottom again. Chill mixture, stirring several times, 30 minutes, or until it mounds lightly on a spoon.

6 While gelatin mixture chills, beat egg whites until foamy-white and double in volume in a medium-size bowl; beat in granulated sugar, 1 tablespoon at a time, beating all the time until meringue stands in firm peaks. Beat ½ cup of the cream until stiff in a small bowl. (Set remaining cream aside for topping.)

7 Fold meringue, then whipped cream into thickened gelatin mixture until no streaks of white remain. Spoon into cooled pastry shell. Chill several hours, or until firm.

8 Just before serving, beat remaining ½ cup cream until stiff in a small bowl; spoon in puffs on top of pie; garnish with orange sections.

Rummy Nesselrode Pie
Bake shell at 425° for 15 minutes. Makes one 9-inch pie

½ package piecrust mix
2 envelopes unflavored gelatin
½ cup sugar
4 eggs, separated
1½ cups milk
¼ cup light rum
¼ teaspoon cream of tartar
1 cup cream for whipping
1 jar (10 ounces) nesselrode dessert sauce
Red food coloring

1 Prepare piecrust mix, following label directions, or make pastry from your favorite single-crust recipe. Roll out to a 12-inch round on a lightly floured pastry cloth or board; fit into a 9-inch pie plate. Trim overhang to ½ inch; turn edge under, flush with rim; flute to make a stand-up edge. Prick shell well all over with a fork.

2 Bake in hot oven (425°) 15 minutes, or until pastry is golden; cool.

3 Mix gelatin and ¼ cup of the sugar in a medium-size saucepan; beat in egg yolks, then milk.

4 Cook slowly, stirring constantly, until gelatin dissolves and mixture thickens slightly; pour into a large bowl. Stir in rum.

5 Place bowl in a deep pan of ice and water to speed setting. Chill, stirring several times, just until as thick as unbeaten egg white.

6 While gelatin mixture chills, beat egg whites with cream of tartar until foamy-white and double in volume in a medium-size bowl. Beat in remaining ¼ cup sugar, 1 tablespoon at a time, until meringue stands in firm peaks. Beat cream until stiff in a bowl.

7 Stir nesselrode sauce and a few drops food coloring into thickened gelatin mixture; fold in meringue, then whipped cream. Spoon into cooled pastry shell. Chill.

8 Just before serving, garnish with puffs of whipped cream and frosted grapes, if you wish. (To fix grapes: Beat 1 egg white slightly with ½ teaspoon water in a small bowl. Dip 1 or 2 small bunches of green grapes into egg-white mixture, then sprinkle with sugar. Place on paper toweling until dry.)

Rosé Chiffon Pie
Bake shell at 350° for 10 minutes. Makes one 9-inch pie

2 cans (4½ ounces each) whole blanched almonds, ground (2 cups)
2 tablespoons butter or margarine, softened
3 tablespoons sugar (for crust)
1 envelope unflavored gelatin
¾ cup sugar (for filling)
4 eggs, separated
½ cup rosé wine
¼ cup water
¼ teaspoon cream of tartar
1 cup cream for whipping
5 drops red food coloring

1 Blend almonds, butter or margarine and the 3 tablespoons sugar in a small bowl. Press evenly over bottom and side of a very lightly buttered 9-inch pie plate.

2 Bake in moderate oven (350°) 10 minutes, or until lightly golden. Cool completely on a wire rack.

3 Mix gelatin and ½ cup of the sugar in the top of a double-boiler; beat in egg yolks until light and fluffy; blend in wine and water; place over simmering water. Cook, stirring constantly, until gelatin dissolves and mixture coats a spoon; pour into a large bowl.

4 Set bowl in a pan of ice and water to speed setting. Chill at room temperature, stirring often, just until as thick as unbeaten egg white.

5 While gelatin mixture chills, beat egg whites with cream of tartar until foamy-white and double in volume in a medium-size bowl; beat in

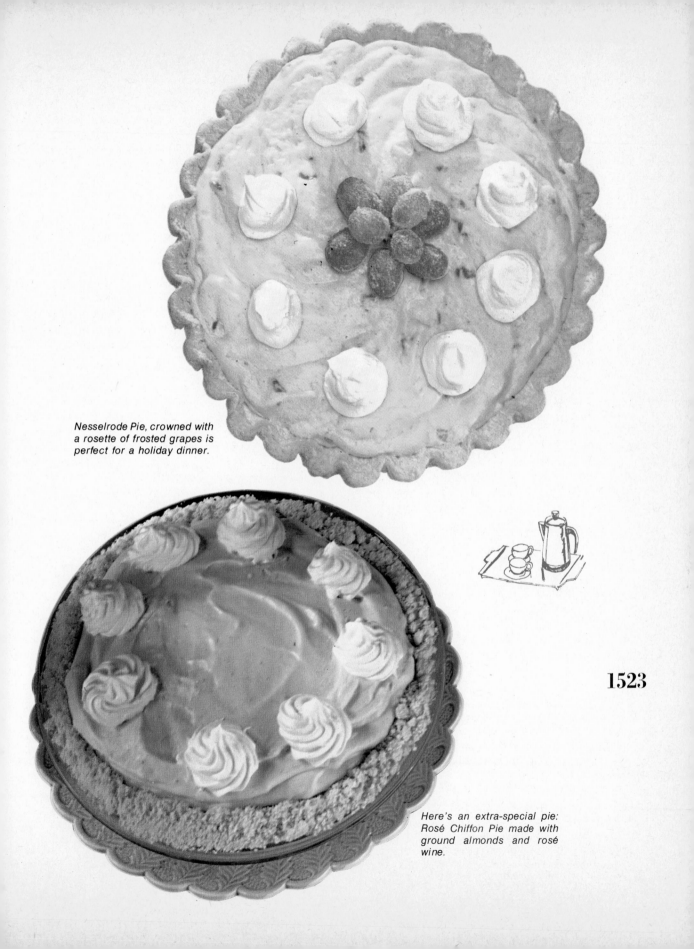

Nesselrode Pie, crowned with a rosette of frosted grapes is perfect for a holiday dinner.

1523

Here's an extra-special pie: Rosé Chiffon Pie made with ground almonds and rosé wine.

Coffee Brittle Pie provides unusual textural contrast: crisp pastry, foamy filling and crunchy brittle.

1524

remaining ¼ cup sugar, 1 tablespoon at a time, beating all the time, until meringue stands in firm peaks. Beat cream until stiff in a second medium-size bowl.

6 Fold meringue, then whipped cream into thickened gelatin mixture until no streaks of white remain; fold in about 5 drops of food coloring to tint pink. Chill again, if necessary, until thick enough to mound when spooned. Spoon into cooled crust. Chill at least 4 hours, or until firm. Just before serving, garnish with whipped cream, if you wish.

●

Heavenly Hawaiian Cream Pie
Golden pineapple, red cherries and snowy marshmallows blend with lots of cream in this billowy chiffonlike treat.
Bake shell at 425° for 15 minutes. Makes one 9-inch pie

1 recipe PLAIN PASTRY I (recipe precedes)
1 can (about 1 pound, 5 ounces) pineapple tidbits
1 envelope unflavored gelatin
¼ cup quartered drained maraschino cherries
2 cups tiny marshmallows (from an about-6-ounce package)
1 cup cream for whipping
½ teaspoon vanilla

1 Prepare pastry, following recipe, or use ½ package piecrust mix, following label directions.
2 Roll out to a 12-inch round on a lightly floured pastry cloth or board; fit into a 9-inch pie plate. Trim overhang to ½ inch; turn under, flush with rim; flute to make a stand-up edge. Prick well all over with a fork.
3 Bake in hot oven (425°) 15 minutes, or until golden; cool completely on a wire rack.
4 Drain syrup from pineapple tidbits into a

2-cup measure; add water, if needed, to make 1¼ cups.

5 Soften gelatin in ½ cup of the pineapple syrup in a small saucepan; heat slowly, stirring constantly, just until gelatin dissolves. Pour into a medium-size bowl.

6 Stir in remaining ¾ cup syrup, pineapple tidbits, cherries and marshmallows. Chill 30 minutes, or until as thick as unbeaten egg white.

7 Beat cream with vanilla until stiff in a small bowl; fold into thickened gelatin mixture. Spoon into cooled pastry shell. Garnish with quarters of maraschino cherries arranged in flower designs, if you wish.

8 Chill several hours, or until firm.

Coffee-Brittle Pie
Bake shell at 425° for 15 minutes. Makes one 9-inch pie

½ *package piecrust mix*
1½ *cups sugar*
¼ *cup water*
½ *cup sliced blanched almonds*
2 *envelopes unflavored gelatin*
1 *tablespoon instant coffee powder*
4 *eggs, separated*
2 *cups milk*
1 *cup cream for whipping*

1 Prepare piecrust mix, following label directions, or make pastry from your favorite single-crust recipe. Roll out to a 12-inch round on a lightly floured pastry cloth or board; fit into a 9-inch pie plate. Trim overhang to ½ inch; turn under, flush with rim; flute to make a stand-up edge. Prick shell well all over with a fork.

2 Bake in hot oven (425°) 15 minutes, or until golden; cool completely in pie plate on a wire rack.

3 Combine 1 cup of the sugar and water in a medium-size saucepan; heat, stirring constantly, until sugar dissolves, then cook, without stirring, until mixture starts to turn golden. Sprinkle almonds into syrup. (Do not stir in.) Continue cooking until richly golden. Pour onto a lightly greased large cookie sheet; spread into a thin layer. Let stand until cool and firm.

4 Mix ¼ cup of the remaining sugar, gelatin and instant coffee powder in a medium-size saucepan; beat in egg yolks; stir in milk.

5 Cook slowly, stirring constantly, until gelatin dissolves. (Do not allow mixture to boil.) Pour into a large bowl. Place bowl in a pan of ice and water to speed setting. Chill, stirring often, just until as thick as unbeaten egg white.

6 While gelatin mixture chills, finely crush enough of the almond mixture to measure ½ cup.

7 Beat egg whites until foamy-white and double in volume in a medium-size bowl; beat in remaining ¼ cup sugar, 1 tablespoon at a time, until meringue stands in firm peaks. Beat ½ cup of the cream until stiff in a small bowl.

8 Fold meringue, then crushed almond mixture and whipped cream into thickened gelatin mixture; pour into prepared shell. Chill several hours, or until firm.

9 Just before serving, beat remaining ½ cup cream until stiff in a small bowl. Break remaining almond mixture into small pieces. Spoon whipped cream into pastry bag fitted with notched tip. Press decorative border around edge on pie. Garnish with almond pieces.

Black Bottom Chiffon Pie
Bake shell at 350° for 8 minutes. Makes one 9-inch pie

1¼ *cups fine chocolate wafer crumbs*
4 *tablespoons (½ stick) butter or margarine*
1 *envelope unflavored gelatin*
¼ *cup water*
¾ *cup sugar*
1 *tablespoon cornstarch*
4 *eggs, separated*
2 *cups light cream or table cream*
2 *squares unsweetened chocolate, melted*
1 *teaspoon vanilla*
¼ *cup light rum*
¼ *teaspoon cream of tartar*

1 Blend wafer crumbs and butter or margarine in a small bowl; press over bottom and side of a lightly buttered 9-inch pie plate.

2 Bake in moderate oven (350°) 8 minutes. Cool completely in pie plate on a wire rack.

3 Sprinkle gelatin over water in a cup; let stand to soften gelatin.

4 Mix ⅓ cup of the sugar and cornstarch in the top of a double boiler; beat in egg yolks; stir in cream. Place over hot, not boiling, water.

5 Cook, stirring constantly, until mixture thickens slightly and coats spoon. Measure out 1 cup of the custard mixture and stir into chocolate in a small bowl; stir in vanilla. Pour into cooled shell. Chill until layer is firm.

6 Stir softened gelatin into remaining custard in top of double boiler; continue heating until gelatin dissolves. Pour into a large bowl.

7 Place bowl in a pan of ice and water; chill, stirring several times, just until as thick as unbeaten egg white; stir in rum.

8 While gelatin mixture chills, beat egg whites with cream of tartar until foamy-white in a medium-size bowl; slowly beat in remaining ¼ cup sugar, 1 tablespoon at a time, until meringue stands in firm peaks. Fold into thickened gelatin

1525

mixture. Spoon on top of chocolate layer in shell. Chill several hours, or until firm. Just before serving, garnish with whipped cream and shaved chocolate.

Most Divine Triple Chocolate Pie
Crisp crust, velvety-smooth filling, creamy topping are all delectably chocolatey.
Makes one 9-inch pie

- 1 baked 9-inch CHOCOLATE SHELL (recipe follows)
- 1 envelope unflavored gelatin
- ¼ cup sugar (for filling)
- ¼ teaspoon salt
- 1 teaspoon instant coffee powder
- 1 cup milk
- 3 egg yolks, beaten
- 3 squares unsweetened chocolate
- ½ teaspoon vanilla
- 3 egg whites
- ¼ teaspoon cream of tartar
- ¼ cup sugar (for meringue)
- 2 cups cream for whipping
- ½ square semisweet chocolate

1 Make and bake CHOCOLATE SHELL; cool.

2 Mix gelatin, ¼ cup sugar, salt and instant coffee powder in large heavy saucepan; blend in milk and beaten egg yolks; add unsweetened chocolate.

3 Heat slowly, stirring constantly, until chocolate is melted and mixture slightly thickened. (Do not let it boil.)

4 Pour into a large bowl; add vanilla and stir until smooth and blended. Cool till mixture mounds.

5 Beat egg whites with cream of tartar until foamy in medium-size bowl; beat in ¼ cup sugar, 1 tablespoon at a time, until meringue stands in stiff peaks.

6 Beat 1 cup cream until stiff in second bowl, using same beater. (Save remaining 1 cup cream for topping.) Beat cooled chocolate mixture until smooth; fold in meringue, then fold in whipped cream.

7 Pour into baked CHOCOLATE SHELL. Chill until firm enough to hold its shape when cut.

8 Beat remaining 1 cup cream until stiff in small bowl; mound on pie. Grate semisweet chocolate over.

CHOCOLATE SHELL—Cut ⅓ cup shortening into 1 cup all-purpose sifted flour and ¼ teaspoon salt in small bowl. Stir in ½ square semisweet chocolate, grated; sprinkle 2 tablespoons water

Most Divine Triple Chocolate Pie puts chocolate in the crust, chocolate in the filling and chocolate on top.

Black Bottom Chiffon Pie is many layered and many splendored. The crust is made of chocolate cookie crumbs. The filling is half rum, half chocolate.

over. Mix lightly just until dough holds together. Roll out and line a 9-inch pie plate; flute edge. Bake in hot oven (400°) about 12 minutes.

Chocolate Chiffon Pie
Makes one 9-inch pie

1 envelope unflavored gelatin
¾ cup sugar
2 cups milk
4 squares unsweetened chocolate
4 eggs, separated
1 teaspoon vanilla
1 nine-inch baked pastry shell
1 cup cream for whipping
1 milk-chocolate candy bar

1 Mix gelatin and sugar in a medium-size saucepan; stir in milk until well blended; add chocolate squares.
2 Cook, stirring constantly, until gelatin dissolves and chocolate melts. Remove saucepan from heat.
3 Beat egg yolks with a fork in a small bowl; gradually beat a generous ½ cup of hot chocolate mixture into eggs. Stir back into saucepan.
4 Cook, stirring constantly, about 3 minutes, or until mixture thickens. Remove from heat and stir in vanilla. Pour into a bowl. Chill about 1 hour, or until cold.
5 Beat the egg whites in a small bowl of mixer at high speed until they are stiff but not dry.
6 Fold egg whites into cold chocolate mixture with wire whip or rubber scraper until well blended. Pour into baked pastry shell.
7 Chill at least 4 hours, or overnight. Just before serving, beat cream until stiff in a small bowl. Top pie with whipped cream and cut curls of chocolate from candy bar to garnish.

1527

Ruffled Chocolate-Mint Pie
Bake shell at 425° for 15 minutes. Makes one 9-inch pie

½ package piecrust mix
1 envelope unflavored gelatin
¾ cup sugar
⅛ teaspoon salt

3 eggs, separated
1 cup milk
2 packages (6 ounces each) semisweet-
chocolate-mint pieces
1 cup cream for whipping

1 Prepare piecrust mix, following label directions, or make pastry from your favorite one-crust recipe. Roll out to a 12-inch round on a lightly floured pastry cloth or board; fit into a 9-inch pie plate. Trim overhang to ½ inch; turn edge under, flush with rim; flute to make a stand-up edge. Prick shell well all over with a fork.
2 Bake in hot oven (425°) 15 minutes, or until pastry is golden; cool completely in pie plate on a wire rack.
3 Mix gelatin, ½ cup of the sugar and salt in the top of a double boiler; beat in egg yolks, then milk. Cook over hot (not boiling) water until mixture thickens slightly and coats spoon; remove from heat but leave over hot water. Stir in chocolate pieces until melted. Pour into a large bowl.
4 Place bowl in a pan of ice and water to speed setting. Chill, stirring often, just until completely cold and thickened slightly.
5 While gelatin mixture chills, beat egg whites until foamy-white in a small bowl; beat in remaining ¼ cup sugar until meringue forms soft peaks. Beat cream until stiff in a medium-size bowl.
6 Fold meringue, then whipped cream into thickened chocolate mixture until no streaks of white remain. Spoon into pastry shell. Chill several hours, or until firm.
7 Just before serving, garnish with more whipped cream and halved thin chocolate mints, if you wish.

CHEESE PIES

1528

Lemon Cheese Pie
Just like the richest cheesecake with a sour-cream topping—and so worth every calorie-packed bite.
Bake at 425° for 10 minutes, then at 350° for 50 minutes. Makes one 9-inch pie

1 recipe PLAIN PASTRY I (recipe precedes)
2 packages (8 ounces each) cream cheese
1 cup sugar (for filling)
3 eggs
1 teaspoon grated lemon peel
2 tablespoons lemon juice

1 cup (8-ounce carton) dairy sour cream
2 tablespoons sugar (for topping)
1 teaspoon vanilla

1 Prepare PLAIN PASTRY I, following recipe, or use ½ package piecrust mix, following label directions. Roll out to a 12-inch round on a lightly floured pastry cloth or board; fit into a 9-inch pie plate. Trim overhang to ½ inch; turn under, flush with rim; flute to make a stand-up edge.
2 Soften cream cheese in a large bowl. Beat in the 1 cup sugar until fluffy, then eggs, 1 at a time, until creamy-smooth; stir in lemon peel and juice. Pour into prepared pastry shell.
3 Bake in hot oven (425°) 10 minutes; lower heat to moderate (350°). Bake 50 minutes longer; remove from oven; turn off heat.
4 While pie bakes, mix sour cream, the 2 tablespoons sugar and vanilla in a small bowl; spread evenly on top of hot pie. Return to oven; let stand 1 hour *with heat off.* Cool completely on a wire rack.

Strawberry Glazed Cheese Pie
Bake at 250° 1 hour. Makes 10 servings, 177 calories each

GRAHAM CRACKER CRUST (recipe follows)
½ cup water
½ cup instant nonfat dry milk (powder)
½ cup sugar
4 eggs
¼ teaspoon salt
1 tablespoon lemon juice
1 teaspoon vanilla
¼ cup sifted all-purpose flour
1 pound cottage cheese
JEWELED FRUIT GLAZE (recipe follows)

1 Prepare a 9-inch pie plate, using GRAHAM CRACKER CRUST.
2 Combine water, dry milk powder, sugar, eggs, salt, lemon juice, vanilla, flour and cottage cheese in container of electric blender; whirl until smooth. (Or you may sieve cheese into a bowl, add remaining ingredients, then beat with a rotary beater until smooth.) Pour into prepared crust.
3 Bake in very slow oven (250°) for 1 hour. Turn oven off and leave pie in oven for 1 hour longer, then remove from oven; cool.
4 Top cooled pie with JEWELED FRUIT GLAZE. Chill until glaze is set.
  GRAHAM CRACKER CRUST—Grease side and

Strawberry Glazed Cheese pie is truly low-calorie.

1 Blend cracker crumbs with 2 tablespoons sugar and butter in a bowl; press ½ cup over bottom of an 8-inch spring-form pan.

2 Mix gelatin and 4 tablespoons sugar in a saucepan; beat in milk and egg yolks. Cook, stirring constantly, until gelatin dissolves; remove from heat. Blend in cream cheese and lemon juice until smooth. Chill, stirring often, until mixture mounds lightly.

3 Beat egg whites until foamy in a bowl; beat in remaining 4 tablespoons sugar until meringue stands in firm peaks. Fold meringue, then cream into gelatin mixture; pour into prepared pan. Sprinkle remaining crumb mixture on top. Chill until firm. Cut into wedges.

ICE CREAM, ANGEL AND OTHER SPECIALTY PIES

Pumpkin Sundae Pie
What a show-off for the effort! Layer filling over ice cream, freeze, then top with more ice cream and sparkly caramel sauce.
Bake at 425° for 15 minutes. Makes one 9-inch pie

   1 *stick piecrust mix*
     OR: 1 recipe PLAIN PASTRY I *(recipe precedes)*
1¼ *cups sugar*
   1 *cup canned pumpkin*
   1 *teaspoon pumpkin-pie spice*
 ½ *teaspoon salt*
   1 *cup cream for whipping*
   2 *pints vanilla ice cream*
    REGAL CARAMEL SAUCE *(recipe follows)*

1 Prepare piecrust mix, following label directions, or make PLAIN PASTRY I. Roll out to a 12-inch round on lightly floured pastry cloth or board; fit into a 9-inch pie plate. Trim overhang to ½ inch; turn under, flush with rim; flute to make a stand-up edge. Prick shell well all over with a fork.

2 Bake in hot oven (425°) 15 minutes, or until golden; cool completely on wire rack.

3 Combine sugar, pumpkin, pumpkin-pie spice and salt in medium-size bowl. Beat cream until stiff in small bowl; fold into pumpkin mixture until no streaks of white remain.

4 Spoon 1½ pints of ice cream into cooled pastry shell. (Save remaining ½ pint for next step.) Top with pumpkin-cream mixture, making soft swirls all over with back of spoon. Freeze at least 2 hours, or until firm.

bottom of pan recommended in recipe with 1 tablespoon butter or margarine (or 2 tablespoons diet margarine). Sprinkle with ½ cup graham cracker crumbs; press firmly into place. Chill 1 hour, or until firm.

JEWELED FRUIT GLAZE—Wash and hull 1 pint of strawberries. Leave whole or cut in half lengthwise. Arrange on top of pie, cut side down. Blend 1 tablespoon cornstarch with 1 cup of water in a small saucepan. Cook over low heat, stirring constantly, until clear and thickened. Add enough liquid sweetener to equal ½ cup sugar. Stir in a few drops red food coloring. Cool slightly. Spoon over strawberries.

VARIATIONS—Canned, water-pack pitted red cherries, frozen or fresh blueberries or canned pineapple chunks packed in juice may be glazed the same way.

Chantilly Cheese Pie
Heavenly smooth and light with lavish lacings of cream cheese and whipped cream.
Makes one 8-inch pie

 ¾ *cup graham cracker crumbs*
10 *tablespoons sugar*
  3 *tablespoons butter or margarine, melted*
  1 *envelope unflavored gelatin*
  1 *cup milk*
  2 *eggs, separated*
  2 *packages (8 ounces each) cream cheese, cut up*
  3 *tablespoons lemon juice*
1½ *cups cream for whipping, whipped*

Frozen Pumpkin Pie, circled with mini pralines (left) and (right) not-much-more-than-bite-size Peach Twinkles.

5 When ready to serve, spoon remaining ice cream in a ring on top; drizzle with part of REGAL CARAMEL SAUCE. Serve with additional sauce.

REGAL CARAMEL SAUCE—Blend 1 cup firmly packed brown sugar, ½ cup light corn syrup and ½ cup water in small saucepan. Heat to boiling; cook, uncovered, 5 minutes. Remove from heat; stir in 1 teaspoon vanilla. Serve warm or cold. Makes 1½ cups.

1530

Frozen Pumpkin Pie

Melt-in-your-mouth pecan candy circles the top of spicy pumpkin cream frozen in a butter-pecan ice cream shell.
Makes one 9-inch pie

2 pints butter-pecan ice cream
1 cup canned pumpkin
¾ cup firmly packed brown sugar (for filling)
½ teaspoon salt
½ teaspoon pumpkin-pie spice
1 teaspoon vanilla
1 cup cream for whipping

2 tablespoons brown sugar (for topping)
2 tablespoons butter or margarine
¼ cup chopped pecans

1 Spoon 1 pint of the ice cream into bottom of a 9-inch pie plate; place spoonfuls of remaining, petal fashion, around edge to make a "shell." Freeze while making filling.
2 Mix pumpkin, ¾ cup brown sugar, salt, pumpkin-pie spice and vanilla in a medium-size bowl.
3 Measure 1 tablespoon of the cream into a small saucepan and set aside for next step. Beat remaining until stiff in a small bowl; fold into pumpkin mixture. Spoon into ice cream shell; freeze while making topping.
4 Combine the 2 tablespoons brown sugar and butter or margarine with cream in saucepan; heat to boiling, then cook 1 minute. Remove from heat; stir in pecans; cool to lukewarm.
5 Spoon pecan mixture in a ring on top of pie. Freeze 3 hours, or until firm. So pie will cut neatly, remove from freezer and let stand at room temperature 15 minutes before serving.

Brazilian Brittle Cream Pie

Royally rich! Bake the shell, pile high with filling of fluffy cream and peanut brittle—and let your freezer do the rest.

Bake shell at 425° for 15 minutes. Makes one 9-inch pie

1 recipe PLAIN PASTRY I (recipe precedes)
2 cups cream for whipping
1 tablespoon instant coffee powder
1 teaspoon vanilla
1½ cups crushed peanut-brittle candy (about ½ pound)

1 Prepare PLAIN PASTRY I, following recipe, or use ½ package piecrust mix, following label directions.
2 Roll out to a 12-inch round on a lightly floured pastry cloth or board; fit into a 9-inch pie plate. Trim overhang to ½ inch; turn under, flush with rim; flute to make a stand-up edge. Prick well all over with a fork.
3 Bake in hot oven (425°) 15 minutes, or until golden; cool completely on a wire rack.
4 Beat cream with instant coffee powder and vanilla until stiff in a large bowl; fold in crushed peanut brittle. Spoon into cooled pastry shell; sprinkle more crushed peanut brittle over top, if you wish.
5 Freeze 3 hours, or until firm.

Blackberry Pie Jubilee

Jumbo berries are combined with currant sauce for the fresh-tasting topper.

Bake shell at 425° for 12 minutes. Makes one 10-inch pie

1 package piecrust mix
1 tablespoon sugar
1 cup fresh currants
2 cups (1 pint) blackberries or boysenberries
¾ cup sugar
¼ cup water
2 pints vanilla ice cream

1 Combine piecrust mix and sugar in a medium-size bowl; prepare, following label directions.
2 Roll out to a 13-inch round on a lightly floured pastry cloth or board; fit into a 10-inch pie plate. Trim overhang to ½ inch; turn under, flush with rim; flute to make a stand-up edge. Prick shell well all over with a fork; brush lightly with milk and sprinkle with sugar, if you wish. (Reroll trimmings and bake for nibbles.)
3 Bake in hot oven (425°) 12 minutes, or until golden; cool completely on a wire rack.
4 Wash currants and remove any large stems; wash blackberries and place in a medium-size bowl. Combine currants with sugar and water in a small saucepan. Heat, stirring constantly,

A sensational summer pie: Blackberry Pie Jubilee made with vanilla ice cream and fresh blackberries.

1531

to boiling, then cook, uncovered, stirring several times, 10 minutes, or until thickened. Press through a sieve into a medium-size bowl, discarding seeds. Pour over blackberries; chill.

5 When ready to serve, spoon ice cream, petal fashion, into cooled pastry shell; top with part of the berry sauce; serve remaining sauce separately.

Ribbon Parfait Pie

Even dessert goes "pizza" style—with a rich cookie crust, ice-cream filling, and colorful fruit topping.

Bake at 375° for 15 minutes. Makes 8 servings

    2 cups sifted all-purpose flour
    ½ cup sugar
    ½ cup (1 stick) butter or margarine
    1 egg, slightly beaten
    1 package (3 ounces) lemon-flavor gelatin
    1¼ cups hot water
    1 pint vanilla ice cream
    2 medium-size firm ripe bananas
    1 can (about 11 ounces) mandarin-orange
        segments, drained
    1 cup green grapes, halved
    5 maraschino cherries, halved
    24 small pecan halves

1 Sift flour and sugar into a medium-size bowl; cut in butter or margarine. Stir in egg until pastry holds together.

2 Press evenly over bottom and up side of a 14-inch pizza pan; flute edge. Prick shell well all over.

3 Bake in moderate oven (375°) 15 minutes, or until golden. Cool completely in pan on a wire rack.

4 Dissolve gelatin in hot water in a medium-size bowl; stir in ice cream, a big spoonful at a time, until completely melted; pour into cooled pastry shell. Chill until firm.

5 Just before serving, peel bananas and slice diagonally. Arrange in rows over filling to divide into four sections. Fill in sections with rows of mandarin-orange segments, and rings of grapes, cherries and pecans. Cut in wedges.

Strawberry Angel Tarts

Crisp meringue shells hold a custardy filling and rosy whole berries.

Bake at 275° for 45 minutes. Makes 8 tarts

    3 eggs
    ½ teaspoon cream of tartar
    ⅛ teaspoon salt
    1 teaspoon vanilla
    ¾ cup sugar (for shells)
    2 tablespoons sugar (for custard)
    1 cup milk
    ½ cup cream for whipping
    2 cups (1 pint) strawberries, washed and hulled

1 Line a large cookie sheet with brown paper; draw eight 3-inch circles, about an inch apart, on paper.

The secret ingredient of Ribbon Parfait Pie is vanilla ice cream, melted and then set with gelatin. Arranging the fruit on top is like painting a canvas.

Strawberry Angel Tarts have crisp meringue crusts.

2 Separate eggs, placing whites in a large bowl and yolks in the top of a double boiler. Add cream of tartar, salt and ½ teaspoon of the vanilla to whites; beat until foamy-white and double in volume.
3 Beat in the ¾ cup sugar, 1 tablespoon at a time, beating all the time until sugar dissolves completely and meringue stands in firm peaks. (Beating will take about 25 minutes in all with an electric beater.)
4 Spoon inside circles on cookie sheet; spread to edges; hollow centers to make shells.
5 Bake in very slow oven (275°) 45 minutes, or until crisp and pale golden. Cool a few minutes on cookie sheet on a wire rack, then peel paper from meringues; cool meringues completely.
6 Add the 2 tablespoons sugar and milk to egg yolks in top of double boiler; beat slightly. Cook, stirring constantly, over simmering water 15 minutes, or until custard thickens slightly and coats a metal spoon. Strain into a small bowl; stir in remaining ½ teaspoon vanilla; chill.
7 About two hours before serving, spoon into shells; chill again.
8 Beat cream until stiff in a small bowl; spoon over custard filling, then arrange strawberries on top.

Chocolate Cordial Pie
Bake shell at 275° for 1 hour. Makes one 9-inch pie

 4 egg whites
¼ teaspoon cream of tartar
¼ teaspoon salt
½ teaspoon vanilla
 1 cup sugar
½ cup maraschino cherries, drained and quartered
 2 tablespoons cherry liqueur (a cordial)

 2 envelopes unflavored gelatin
¾ cup water
 2 pints chocolate ice cream
½ cup cream for whipping
   Red food coloring

1 Generously butter a 9-inch pie plate.
2 Beat egg whites with cream of tartar, salt and vanilla until foamy-white and double in volume in a large bowl. Beat in sugar, 1 tablespoon at a time, beating all the time until sugar dissolves completely and meringue stands in firm peaks. (Beating will take about 25 minutes in all with an electric beater.)
3 Spoon meringue into pie plate; spread almost to side of plate, hollowing center and building up edge slightly to form a shell.
4 Bake in very slow oven (275°) 1 hour, or until firm and lightly golden. Cool completely in pie plate on a wire rack.
5 Combine cherries with cherry liqueur in a small bowl; let stand to season.
6 Soften gelatin in water in a medium-size saucepan; heat slowly, stirring constantly, until gelatin dissolves; pour into a large bowl. Stir in cherry mixture, then beat in ice cream, a few spoonfuls at a time; pour into meringue shell. Chill several hours, or until firm.
7 Just before serving, combine cream and a few drops food coloring in a small bowl; beat until stiff. Spoon into pastry bag fitted with notched tip. Press puffs on top of pie. Garnish with remaining cherries.

Valentine Hearts
Puffs of pink cream fill dainty soft meringue tarts.
Bake at 250° for 1 hour. Makes 8 tarts

 4 egg whites
¼ teaspoon cream of tartar
¼ teaspoon salt
 1 cup sugar
   STRAWBERRY SNOW *(recipe follows)*

1 Beat egg whites with cream of tartar and salt until foamy-white in a large bowl. Sprinkle in sugar *very slowly*, 1 tablespoon at a time, beating all the time until meringue stands in firm peaks.
2 Draw eight 5-inch heart outlines, 2 inches apart, on brown-paper-lined cookie sheets; spread ½ cup meringue inside each; dish centers.
3 Bake in very slow oven (250°) 1 hour, or until pale golden. Cool 5 minutes; remove carefully; cool completely.

1533

PIES THEY'LL APPLAUD

Strawberry Snow
Pink and light and so wonderfully rich!
Makes enough to fill 8 tarts

4 egg yolks
1 whole egg
1 tablespoon sugar
1 teaspoon lemon juice
1 package (10 ounces) frozen strawberries, thawed
  Red food coloring
1 cup cream for whipping

1 Beat egg yolks and whole egg slightly in top of a small double boiler; stir in sugar, lemon juice and thawed strawberries.
2 Cook, stirring constantly, over simmering water, 15 minutes, or until thick. Tint deeper pink with food coloring; chill well.
3 Beat cream until stiff in a small bowl; fold half into strawberry mixture; spoon into tart shells. Chill at least 4 hours. Tint remaining whipped cream with food coloring; swirl on top.

When You Make Valentine Hearts:
Spoon meringue inside outlines on brown paper, then spread to cover completely. Hollow the center of each with a spoon, building up edge evenly to form a "dish" for filling. It's a good idea to start with a pattern—cut the easy way from folded paper—so baked meringues will all be the same size.

Mystery Lemon Pie-Cake
The mystery? The topping bakes on the bottom of the pastry shell, and the cake bobs to the top.
Bake at 350° for 1 hour. Makes one 9-inch pie

½ package piecrust mix
1¼ cups sugar
2 tablespoons cornstarch
2 eggs
¼ cup bottled lemon juice
¾ cup water
1 tablespoon butter or margarine
1¼ cups sifted cake flour
1 teaspoon baking powder
½ teaspoon salt
¼ cup soft vegetable shortening
½ cup milk

1 Prepare piecrust mix, following label directions, or make pastry from your own favorite one-crust recipe. Roll out to a 12-inch round on a lightly floured pastry cloth or board; fit into a 9-inch pie plate. Trim overhang to ½ inch; turn under, flush with rim; flute to make a high stand-up edge. Chill while mixing up the topping and cake batter.
2 Mix ½ cup of the sugar and cornstarch in a medium-size saucepan. Beat in 1 of the eggs, lemon juice and water. (Remaining ¾ cup sugar and egg are for cake batter.)
3 Cook, stirring constantly, until mixture thickens and boils 3 minutes; stir in butter or margarine. Cool to lukewarm while mixing cake batter.
4 Sift cake flour, remaining ¾ cup sugar, baking powder and salt into a medium-size bowl; add vegetable shortening and milk. Beat with an electric beater at medium speed 2 minutes, or 200 strokes by hand. Add remaining egg; beat 1 minute longer, or 100 strokes.
5 Pour into chilled pastry shell; drizzle cooled lemon topping over batter to cover completely.
6 Bake in moderate oven (350°) 1 hour, or until top turns golden and springs back when lightly pressed with fingertip. Let cool on a wire rack. Serve warm, plain or with ice cream or cream, if you wish.

1534

INDEX TO RECIPES IN THIS VOLUME

1535